AF600622

ALTARS ACCORDING TO THE CODE OF CANON LAW

THE CATHOLIC UNIVERSITY OF AMERICA
CANON LAW STUDIES
NUMBER 38

ALTARS ACCORDING TO THE CODE OF CANON LAW

A DISSERTATION

Submitted to the Faculty of Canon Law of the Catholic University of America in partial fulfillment of the requirements for the Degree of Doctor of Canon Law

BY
NICHOLAS MARTIN BLILEY, O. S. B., J. C. L.,
Belmont Abbey, Belmont, N. C.

THE CATHOLIC UNIVERSITY OF AMERICA
WASHINGTON, D. C.
1927

Nihil Obstat.

✠ THOMAS J. SHANAN, S. T. D.,
Censor Deputatus.
Washington, D. C., May 10, 1927.

Imprimi Permittitur.

✠ VINCENTIUS TAYLOR, O. S. B.,
Abbas-Ordinarius.
Belmont, N. C., May 24, 1927.

Imprimatur.

✠ MICHAEL J. CURLEY,
Archiepiscopus Baltimorensis.
Baltimore, Md., May 31, 1927.

PREFACE

The New Code of Canon Law, codified by command of Pope Pius X and promulgated by Pope Benedict XV, has given a new impetus to the study of the laws of the Church. In every field of the legislation of the Church, studies and investigations are being made to show not only the present extent and force of the law but also the historical development of the law with its various changes and modifications to its present reading and obligation. In this connection it will be interesting and of value to institute a study of the laws of the Church in regard to the altar upon which the most august Sacrifice of the Mass is daily offered. The Code of Canon Law, as officially published, made no important changes in the laws governing the altar, but rather crystallized the legislation already made and brought it together in one place. Before the publication of the Code, the recent legislation regarding altars was found scattered through the various decrees of the Sacred Congregation of Rites and in the instructions of the Congregation for the Propagation of the Faith, and consequently was not readily accessible to all.

The altar occupies the most important place in the church, since upon it the Holy Sacrifice of the Mass, about which Catholic faith centers, is celebrated. Accordingly, the Church has formulated regulations for the construction of the altar which will make it a suitable and worthy place where the Holy Sacrifice may be offered. Every priest or other person concerned in the building of altars, therefore, will be interested in knowing these laws and anxious to carry them out. With a view better to attain this end, this treatise has been written. To make the work complete, not only the canonical laws, but also the liturgical requirements of the Church have been treated at length. However, only the essential elements of the altar itself have been described. A discussion of the reredos, baldachin, tabernacle, and altar-ledge has not been included in this work. Nevertheless, it is the hope of the author that this work may serve a useful purpose in bringing about a better knowledge of the nature of the construction of the altar, especially the fixed altar, and in making it easier for those whose duty it may be to construct altars.

This treatise is likewise limited to the study of the altar of the Latin or Western Church. Whereas reference is made to the altars in the Oriental Churches in the chapter on the terms used to designate altars and in the section on the early history of the altar, no attempt has been made to include in this work a study of the altars of the different Oriental Rites.

The writer takes this opportunity to express his thanks to the faculty of Canon Law of the Catholic University for the many suggestions, criticisms, and aids given in the prepartion of this work.

TABLE OF CONTENTS

PART II

The Legislation of the Code on Altars

SECTION 1

The Fixed Altar

SECTION 2

The Portable Altar

PART III

MISCELLANEA

BIBLIOGRAPHY

Juridical Sources

Acta Apostolicæ Sedis, Rome, 1909—.

Acta Sanctæ Sedis, 41 vols., Rome, 1865-1908.

Cæremoniale Episcoporum Clementis VIII, Innocentii X et Benedicti XIII iussu editum, Benedicti XIV et Leonis XIII auctoritate recognitum, Turin-Rome, 1924.

Canones et Decreta Sacrosancti Oecumenici Concilii Tridentini, Turin, 1913.

Codex Iuris Canonici Pii X Pontificis Maximi iussu digestus Benedicti Papæ XV auctoritate promulgatus, Rome, 1917.

Codicis Iuris Canonici Fontes cura Emi. Petri Card. Gasparri editi, 4 vols., Rome, 1923-1926.

Collectanea S. Congregationis de Propaganda Fide seu Decreta, Instructiones, Rescripta pro Apostolicis Missionibus ex Tabulario eiusdem Sacræ Congregationis deprompta, Rome, 1893.

Collectanea S. Congregationis de Propaganda Fide seu Decreta, Instructiones, Rescripta pro Apostolicis Missionibus, 2 vols., Rome 1907.

Corpus Iuris Cononici, editio Lipsiensis secunda post Aemilii Ludovici Richteri curas ad librorum manu scriptorum et editionis Romanæ fidem recognovit et adnotatione critica instruxit Aemilius Friedberg, 2 vols., Leipsic, 1922.

Decreta Authentica Congregationis Sacrorum Rituum ex Actis eiusdem collecta eiusque auctoritate promulgata sub auspiciis SS. D. N. Leonis Papæ XIII, 6 vols., Rome, 1898-1912.

Decreta Authentica Sacræ Congregationis Indulgentiis Sacrisque Reliquiis præpositæ ab anno 1668 ad annum 1882 edita iussu et auctoritate SS. D. N. Leonis PP. XIII, Ratisbon, 1883.

Gardellini, Aloisius, *Decreta Authentica Congregationis Sacrorum Rituum ex actis eiusdem collecta,* 3. ed., 4 vols., with appendices, Rome, 1856-1887.

Hardouin, Jean, S. I., *Acta Conciliorum et Epistolæ Decretales, ac Constitutiones Summorum Pontificum,* 12 vols., Paris, 1714-1715.

Liber Pontificalis, edited by Mgr. L. Duchesne, 2 vols., Paris, 1886.

Mansi, Ioannes Dominicus, *Sacrorum Conciliorum Nova et Amplissima Collectio,* 59 vols., Paris-Arnhem-Leipsic, 1901-1927.

Missale Romanum ex decreto Sacrosancti Concilii Tridentini restitutum S. Pii V Pontificis Maximi iussu editum aliorum Pontificum cura recognitum a Pio X reformatum et Ssmi. D. N. Benedicti XV auctoritate vulgatum, Rome, 1920.

Pontificale Romanum Summorum Pontificum iussu editum a Benedicto XIV et Leone XIII Pontificibus Maximis recognitum et castigatum, Mechlin, 1895.

Rituale Romanum Pauli V Pontificis Maximi iussu editum a Benedictio XIV et a Pio X castigatum et auctum cui accedunt Benedictionum et Instructionum appendices duæ, Rome, 1913.

Rituale Romanum Pauli V Pontificis Maximi iussu editum aliorumque Pontificum cura recognitum atque auctoritate Ssmi. D. N. Pii Papæ XI ad normam Codicis Iuris Canonici accommodatum, Rome, 1925.

Schneider, Joseph, S. I., *Rescripta Authentica Sacræ Congregationis Indulgentiis Sacrisque Reliquiis præpositæ,* Ratisbon, 1885.

Authors and Periodicals

Aichner, Simon, *Compendium Iuris Ecclesiastici ad usum cleri, ac præsertim per Imperium Austriacum in cura animarum laborantis,* 6. ed., Brixen, 1887.

Alphonsus Liguori, Saint, *Theologia Moralis,* 11. ed., 3 vols., Bassani, 1816.

American Ecclesiastical Review, Philadelphia, 1889—.

Amort, Eusebius, *Elementa Iuris Canonici Veteris et Moderni,* 3 vols., Ferrara, 1763.

Augustine, Charles, O. S. B., *A Commentary on the New Code of Canon Law,* 8 vols., St. Louis, 1918-1922.

Ayrinhac, H. A., S. S., *Constitution of the Church in the New Code of Canon Law,* New York, 1925.

Barbosa, Augustinus, *Iuris Ecclesiastici Universi Libri Tres,* Lyons, 1660.

Bargilliat, M., *Prælectiones Iuris Canonici,* 37. ed., 2 vols., Paris, 1923-1924.

Benedict XIV, *De Sacrosancto Missæ Sacrificio,* Prati, 1843.

——*De Synodo Diœcesana,* 2 vols., Ferrara, 1775.

Beringer, Franz, S. I.-Steinen, P. A., S. I., *Die Ablässe, ihr Wesen und Gebrauch,* 15. ed., 2 vols., Paderborn, 1921-1922.

Bishop, Edmund, "On the History of the Christian Altar," *The Downside Review,* XXIV (1905), 154-182; reprinted by St. Gregory's Society, Downside, Stratton-on-the-Fosse, nr. Bath. (References are made to the reprint.)

Blat, Albertus, O. P., *Commentarium Textus Codicis Iuris Canonici,* 5 vols., Rome, 1921-1924.

Bona, Ioannes Card., Ord. Cist., *Rerum Liturgicarum Libri Duo,* Rome, 1671.

Bouvry, G. F. J., *Expositio Rubricarum Breviarii, Missalis et Ritualis Romani,* 2. ed., 2 vols., Paris, 1864.

Braun, Joseph, S. I., *Der christliche Altar in seiner geschichtlichen Entwicklung,* 2 vols., Munich, 1924.

Cabrol, Fernand, O. S. B., *Dictionnaire l'Archéologie Chrétienne et de Liturgie,* Paris, 1907—.

Cavalieri, Ioannes Michael, O. S. Aug., *Opera Omnia Liturgica seu Commentaria in authentica Sacræ Rituum Congregationis decreta ad Romanum præsertim Breviarium, Missale, et Rituale quomodolibet attinentia,* 5 vols., Venice, 1758.

Cappello, Felix M., S. I., *Tractatus Canonico-Moralis de Sacramentis iuxta Codicem Iuris Canonici,* 3 vols., Turin, 1921-1926.

Catholic Encyclopedia, The, 17 vols., New York, 1907-1922.

Charles Borromeo, Saint, *Instructions on Ecclesiastical Building.* Translated from the original Latin and annoted by George J. Wigley, M. R. I. B. A., London, 1857.

Chelodi, Ioannes, *Ius de Personis,* Trent, 1922.

Cocchi, Guidus, C. M., *Commentarium in Codicem Iuris Canonici ad usum scholarum, Liber III, De Rebus, Pars II, De Locis et Temporibus Sacris, Pars III, De Cultu Divino,* Turin-Rome, 1924.

Corblet, L'Abbé Jules, *Histoire Dogmatique, Liturgique et Archéologique du Sacrement de l'Eucharistie,* 2 vols., Paris, 1885-1886.

Coronata, Matthæus a, O. M. C., *De Locis et Temporibus Sacris,* Turin, 1922.

Corpus Scriptorum Ecclesiasticorum Latinorum, Vienna, 1876—.

De Herdt, P. J. B., *Sacræ Liturgiæ Praxis,* 7. ed., 3 vols., Louvain, 1883.

De Lugo, Ioannes Card., S. I., *Disputationes Scholasticæ et Morales,* 8 vols., Paris, 1868-1869.

De Rossi, G. B., *La Roma Sotterranea Cristiana,* 3 vols., Rome, 1864-1877.

Devoti, Ioannes, *Institutionum Canonicarum Libri IV,* 3 vols., Rome, 1860.

Duchesne, Mgr. L., *Christian Worship: Its Origin and Evolution.* Translated from the third French edition by M. L. McClure. London, 1903.

Durandus, Gulielmus, *Rationale Divinorum Officiorum,* Naples, 1859.

Durantus, Ioannes Stephanus, *De Ritibus Ecclesiæ Catholicæ Libri Tres,* Rome, 1591.

Encyclopædia of Religion and Ethics, edited by James Hastings, M. A., D. D., 12 vols., New York, 1908-1922.

Ephemerides Liturgicæ, Rome, 1887—.

Fanfani, Ludovicus I., O. P., *De Iure Parochorum,* Turin-Rome, 1924.

Ferraris, F. Lucius, O. M. Reg. Obs. S. Francisci, *Bibliotheca Canonica, Iuridica, Moralis, Theologica, necnon Ascetica, Polemica, Rubricistica, Historica,* 9 vols., Rome, 1885-1899.

Gasparri, Petrus, *Tractatus Canonicus de Sanctissima Eucharistia,* 2 vols., Paris, 1897.

Gattico, Ioannes Baptista, *De Oratoriis Domesticis et De Usu Altaris Portatilis,* Rome, 1746.

Gihr, Nicholas, *The Holy Sacrifice of the Mass, Dogmatically, Liturgically and Ascetically Explained.* Translated from the sixth German edition. 5. ed., St. Louis, 1921.

Giraldi, Ubaldus, *Expositio Iuris Pontificii,* 2 vols., Rome, 1829.

Goar, Iacobus, O. P., *Euchologion sive Rituale Græcorum,* Paris, 1647.

Hedley, John Cuthbert, O. S. B., *The Holy Eucharist,* London, 1907.

Hefele, Carl Joseph, *Conciliengeschichte,* 2. ed., 9 vols., Freiburg im Breisgau, 1873-1890.

Kirchenlexikon, 2. ed., 12 vols., Freiburg im Breisgau, 1882-1901.

Kraus, F. X., *Real-Encyklopädie der christlichen Alterthümer,* 2 vols., Freiburg im Breisgau, 1882-1901.

Lowrie, Walter, *Monuments of the Early Church,* New York, 1901.

Many, S., S. S., *Prælectiones de Locis Sacris,* Paris, 1904.

——*Prælectiones de Missa,* Paris, 1903.

Martène, Edmund, O. S. B., *De Antiquis Ecclesiæ Ritibus,* 4 vols., Rouen, 1700-1706.

Martigny, M. L'Abbé, *Dictionnaire des Antiquités Chrétiennes,* Paris, 1877.

Martinucci, Pius-Menghini, I. B. M., *Manuale Sacrarum Cæremoniarum,* 3. ed., 4 vols., Rome, 1911-1913.

Migne, *Patrologia Græca,* 161 vols., Paris, 1857-1866.

Migne, *Patrologia Latina,* 221 vols., Paris, 1844-1855.

Monumenta Germaniæ Historica, Epistolæ, Berlin, 1887—.

Monumenta Germaniæ Historica, Legum Sectio II, Capitularia Regum Francorum, Hanover, 1883—.

Monumenta Germaniæ Historica, Legum Sectio III, Concilia, Hanover, 1903—.

Monumenta Germaniæ Historica, Scriptores Rerum Merovingicarum, Hanover, 1885—.

Muratori, Ludovicus A., *Liturgia Romana Vetus,* 2 vols., Venice, 1748.

Noldin, H., S. I., *De Sacramentis,* 16. ed., Innsbruck, 1923.

O'Brien, John, *A History of the Mass and its Ceremonies in the Eastern and Western Church,* New York, 1879.

Ojetti, Benedictus, S. I., *Synopsis Rerum Moralium et Iuris Pontificii,* 3. ed., 4 vols., Rome, 1909-1914.

Paschang, John Linus, *The Sacramentals,* Washington, 1925.

Pasqualigo, Zacharia, *De Sacrificio Novæ Legis Quæstiones Theologicæ, Morales, Iuridicæ,* 2 vols., Venice, 1707.

Petra, Vincentius Card., *Commentaria ad Constitutiones Apostolicas, seu Bullas Singulas Summorum Pontificum in Bullario Romano contentas secundum Collectionem Cherubini incipientes a Divo Leone Magno,* 5 vols., Venice, 1729.

Pignatelli, Iacobus, *Consultationes Canonicæ,* 11 vols., Geneva, 1700.

Pirhing, Henricus, S. I., *Ius Canonicum Nova Methodo Explicatum, omnibus capitulis titulorum promiscue et confuse positis in ordinem doctrinæ digestis,* 4 vols., Dillingen, 1676.

Probst, Ferdinand, *Liturgie der drei ersten christlichen Jahrhunderten,* Tübingen, 1870.

Prümmer, Dominicus M., O. P., *Manuale Iuris Canonici,* 3. ed., Freiburg im Breisgau, 1922.

Reiffenstuel, Anacletus, O. F. M., *Ius Canonicum Universum,* 4 vols., Venice, 1735.

Renaudot, Eusebius, *Liturgicarum Orientalium Collectio,* 2. ed., 2 vols., Frankfort, 1847.

Rock, Daniel, *Hierurgia; or, The Holy Sacrifice of the Mass,* 3. ed., 2 vols., London, 1892.

——*The Church of our Fathers,* 4 vols., London, 1903.

Rohault de Fleury, Charles, *La Messe, Études Archéologiques sur ses Monuments,* 8 vols., Paris, 1883-1889.

Schmalzgrueber, Franciscus, S. I., *Ius Ecclesiasticum Universum,* 12 vols., Rome, 1843-1845.

Schreiber, Ellis, "The Christian Altar," *The American Catholic Quarterly Review,* Philadelphia, XXXI (1906), 658-667.

Schulte, A. J., *Consecranda,* New York, 1906.

Schuster, Ildefonso, O. S. B., *The Sacramentary (Liber Sacramentorum).* Translated from the Italian by Arthur Levelis-Marke, M. A. Vol. I, New York, 1924.

Smith, William-Cheetham, Samuel, *A Dictionary of Christian Antiquities,* 2 vols., Hartford, 1880.

Suarez, Franciscus, S. I., *Opera Omnia,* 26 vols., Paris, 1856-1859.

Thalhofer, Valentine, *Handbuch der katholischen Liturgik,* 2 vols., Freiburg im Breisgau, 1883-1890.

Thomas Aquinas, Saint, *Opera Omnia,* 34 vols., Paris, 1871-1880.

Van der Stappen, J. F., *Sacra Liturgia,* 2. ed., 5 vols., Mechlin, 1902-1905.

Vermeersch, A., S. I.-Creusen, J., S. I., *Epitome Iuris Canonici cum commentariis ad scholas et ad usum privatum,* 2. ed., 3 vols., Bruges, 1924-1925.

Walsh, Msgr. John, *The Mass and Vestments of the Catholic Church: Liturgical, Doctrinal, Historical and Archæological.* Troy, (N. Y.), 1909.

Wapelhorst, Innocentius, O. F. M., *Compendium Sacræ Liturgiæ,* 9. ed., New York, 1915.

Weber, Edward J., "The Fundamentals of Church Building," article VIII, "Altars," *The Homiletic and Pastoral Review,* New York, XXVII (1927), 857-867.

Wernz, Franciscus X., S. I., *Ius Decretalium,* 3. ed., 6 vols., Rome, 1908-1914.

Winslow, Francis Joseph, *Vicars and Prefects Apostolic,* Washington, 1924.

Woywod, Stanislaus, O. F. M., "The Law of the Code on Altars," *The Homiletic and Pastoral Review,* New York, XXVI (1925), 261-270.

Zitelli, Zephyrinus-Solieri, Franciscus, *Apparatus seu Compendium Iuris Ecclesiastici in usum Episcoporum et Sacerdotum præsertim apostolico munere fulgentium,* Rome, 1907.

Other Authorities, not given in this Bibliography, are mentioned in full in the footnotes in the course of this monograph.

Altars According to the Code of Canon Law

PART I

Preliminary Notions and History

Section 1

Preliminary Notions

CHAPTER I

INTRODUCTION

The altar in the general acceptation of the term is an elevated surface in the form of a table upon which sacrifice is offered to God. Sacrifice is the highest form of worship given to God and consists, according to the proper acceptation of the term, in making an oblation to God of some sensible thing by a lawfully appointed minister, in order to acknowledge, by the destruction or at least the change effected in the offering, the majesty and sovereign power of God and man's absolute dependence upon Him. Nature itself invariably inspired man with the idea that sacrifice is the essential and highest act of external religion. From the world's foundation to the present moment, the existence of sacrifice may be more or less discovered amongst men throughout the earth, however widely separated from each other by almost immeasurable distances, or the interposition of barriers erected by nature. Wherever sacrifices were offered to God, the altar was used as the place of sacrifice. The altar, therefore, is as ancient as sacrifice and dates back to the origin of man.[1]

Sacred Scripture does not mention the existence of any altar before the Deluge, although mention is made of sacrifices being offered to

1 Cf. Thalhofer, *Handbuch der katholischen Liturgik*, I, 747; Rock, *Hierurgia*, I, 159-162.

God by Cain and Abel [2], and many writers are of opinion that sacrifices of some kind were offered by Adam and other antediluvian patriarchs living under the law of nature.[3] The erection of an altar is first mentioned in Holy Scripture when Noe built an altar after the safe delivery from the ark.[4] Thereafter mention is made of altars erected by Abraham [5], Isaac [6], Jacob [7], and Moses.[8] Holy Scripture does not tell us of what material or form these altars of the patriarchs were, but it can be judged from the example of Jacob on the morning after his mysterious dream in setting up a stone and anointing it [9] and from the later prescription of the Mosaic Law [10] that they were elevations made from earth or unhewn stones. These simple structures used as altars were usually erected in places where God had manifested His goodness or a special favor or blessing in some particular manner. The Sacred Books give us precise details only on the altar of incense [11], the table of the loaves of proposition [12], and the altar of holocaust [13], which Moses had constructed in the tabernacle, and which Solomon afterwards placed in the temple at Jerusalem.

These minute regulations pertaining to the altars constructed under the written law of Moses in the Old Dispensation, however, exercised little, if any, influence on the Christian altar. Nor did the pagan altars, so numerous and so varied in form, have any relation with the Christian altar. It cannot be said, therefore, that the Christian altar is a continuation of the Jewish or pagan altar. For the sacrifice of the New Law, so different in its nature from all other sacrifices and so sublime in the Victim offered, new conceptions of detail were needed, and the first Christians must have necessarily sought for them in the Last Supper of our Lord and in the practices of the Apostles. Christ, our Lord and Redeemer, had celebrated the first Eucharistic

---

2 Gen. IV, 3-5.
3 Gattico, *De Usu Alaris Portatilis*, cap. 1, n. 2; Bona, *Rerum Liturgicarum*, lib. I, cap. 20, n. 1.
4 Gen. VIII, 20.
5 Gen. XII, 7-8; XXII, 9.
6 Gen. XXVI, 25.
7 Gen. XXXIII, 20; XXXV, 7.
8 Exod. XVII, 15.
9 Gen. XXVIII, 16-19.
10 Exod. XX, 24-25; cf. Deut. XXVII, 4-7.
11 Exod. XXX, 1-6; XXXVII, 25-28.
12 Exod. XXV, 23-30.
13 Exod. XXVII, 1-8; XXXVIII, 1-7.

sacrifice upon a table, and it was surely also a table which the Apostles in imitation of Him used on their missionary journeys. Thus St. Paul in his first epistle to the Corinthians (X, 21) speaks expressly of a τράπεζα Κυρίου, *mensa Domini,* "table of the Lord." The altar, consequently, is rather an outgrowth of Catholic dogma concerning the Holy Eucharist as the unbloody sacrifice of the New Law and the sacrament wherein the souls of men are replenished with the Body and Blood of Christ, the Savior.[14]

As to the altars of the first three centuries very little information is extant. The altar usually was a table or a structure similar to a table. Origen [15], Hippolytus [16], and Dionysius of Alexandria [17] expressly call the structure upon which the Eucharistic sacrifice is offered τράπεζα, "table,"—the θυσιαστήριον of St. Ignatius and the *altare* of St. Cyprian. The writer of the treatise *De Aleatoribus* calls it *mensa.*[18] Tabular-shaped altars are also represented in the frescos of the catacombs. In the catacombs it was likewise on a table of wood, of stone, or of marble that the sacred mysteries were celebrated; but this table served as a cover of the tomb of the martyr, sometimes inclosed in a niche surmounted by a vault in the form of an arch, called an *arcosolium,* or sometimes set against the wall. In the larger oratories the altar was sometimes a mass of masonry, or again a table, or a marble slab supported by columns. The early Christians in making of the altar and of the tomb of the martyrs only one monument may have been inspired by the passage of the Apocalypse of St. John (VI, 9): "And when he had opened the fifth seal, I saw under the altar the souls of them that were slain for the word of God, and for the testimony which they held."

When peace had been granted the Church by Constantine and the Christians were permitted to build churches in public without being molested, basilicas and chapels were erected in Rome and elsewhere in honor of the most famous martyrs, and the altars, when it was possible, were located directly above their tombs. The practice of celebrating Mass only on altars built above the tombs of martyrs or on altars containing the relics of martyrs became general very early

14 Cf. Corblet, *Histoire du Sacrement de l'Eucharistie,* II, 59; Braun, *Der christliche Altar,* I, 48-50.

15 *Contra Celsum,* lib. VIII, cap. 24, Migne, *P. G.*, XI, 1553.

16 *Fragmenta in Proverbia,* Migne, *P. G.*, X, 628.

17 In Eusebius, *Historia Ecclesiastica,* lib. VII, cap. 9, Migne, *P. G.*, XX, 656.

18 Cap. 11; *Corpus Scriptorum Eccles. Latin.*, III (part 3), 103.

in the development of the altar. This connection of the tomb of the martyrs with the altar gave rise also to the gradual change in the altar from the table form to its tomb-like appearance, especially when it became the general custom to inclose the relics of martyrs and other saints in the support of the altar. This practice has passed into the general law of the Church so that at the present time the altar cannot be validly consecrated without the relics of martyrs unless a dispensation from this requirement is obtained from the Holy See.

The altar has always been required for the celebration of Holy Mass. There never was any exception to this regulation except in cases of absolute necessity. Two remarkable examples are mentioned in history. Philostorgius in his *Ecclesiastica Historia* narrates of St. Lucian, priest and martyr of Antioch (d. 312), that, when he was imprisoned and bound by chains, he offered the Holy Sacrifice reclining on his back and using his own breast as an altar.[19] Theodoret, bishop of Cyrus (d. cir. 457), relates that, when he was asked by the hermit Maris to say Mass in his cell, he celebrated Mass on the hands of deacons as an altar.[20] These examples, Benedict XIV admonishes us [21], are worthy more of our admiration than imitation, because, as he remarks, it has always been the constant discipline of the Church that Mass be celebrated upon an altar. The Holy See will dispense even today in extraordinary cases, especially in missionary countries, from some of the requisites essential to a consecrated altar or altar-stone, but never grants an indult to celebrate Mass without a consecrated altar.[22]

The object of this study is to present in a practical way the legislation of the Church on the altar as it has been brought together in the Code of Canon Law. This legislation is found in the second part of the third book under title eleven, *De Altaribus,* canons 1197 to 1202. In these six canons are summed up the regulations governing the

19 "Cum iam moriturus esset, et tyrannica vis nec Ecclesiæ, nec altaris copiam faceret, cumque vincula et plagæ ne quidem ut se commoveret, ei permitterent, supinum iacentem, supra proprium pectus tremendum sacrificium peregisse, et tum ipsum participasse, tum aliis ut de immaculato sacrificio participarent, copiam fecisse."—Lib. II, cap. 13, Migne, *P. G.,* LXV, 476.

20 "Ego vero libenter obtemperavi, et sacra vasa afferi iussi (nec enim procul aberat locus), diaconorumque manibus utens pro altari, mysterium et divinum ac salutare sacrificium obtuli."—*Historia Religiosa,* cap. 20, Migne, *P. G.,* LXXXII, 1429.

21 *De Sacrificio Missæ,* lib. I, cap. 2, n. 4.

22 Gasparri, *De SS. Eucharistia,* I, n. 311.

erection, consecration, and desecration of the altar. Other canons of the Code are also indirectly connected with the altar as, for example, those granting to Cardinals and other prelates the right of consecrating altars; these canons will likewise be taken into consideration to make this study as complete as possible. A history of the legislation pertaining to the altar has been added as an aid to a full understanding of the development of the altar. These historical data have been placed under a separate heading to avoid any confusion that might arise from a consideration of the history in connection with the present legislation of the Code. Only in instances where some historical point was not touched in this general history, is the history given under the present legislation. Consequently in Part I, after the preliminary considerations in Section 1, the history of the legislation in regard to the altar will be described in Section 2. The legislation of the Code will be treated in Part II; while in Part III, several chapters will be devoted to special matters relating to the altar in general.

CHAPTER II

TERMS USED TO DESIGNATE ALTARS

§ *1. In Holy Scripture*

The words used in Holy Scripture to designate the altar are in the Vulgate *altare, ara,* and *mensa;* in the Greek text, the corresponding names θυσιαστήριον, βωμός, and τράπεζα.

In the Old Testament *altare* almost without exception refers to the altar erected to the true God, whereas *ara* is used to indicate the pagan altar. A good example of this use occurs in the first book of the Machabees (I, 57): *"Die quinta decima mensis casleu, quinto et quadragesimo et centesimo anno, ædificavit rex Antiochus abominandum idolum desolationis super altare Dei; et per universas civitates Iuda in circuitu ædificaverunt aras."* There are, however, a few instances where *altare* is used to designate altars erected to false gods [1] and where *ara,* although less often, is used to indicate altars dedicated to the one true God.[2] In the New Testament *ara* is used only once and then to designate the pagan altar found by St. Paul at Athens.[3] *Altare* in the sense of the Christian altar is used only in the epistle of St. Paul to the Hebrews (XIII, 10): *"Habemus altare, de quo edere non habent potestatem qui tabernaculo deserviunt."* Catholic theologians do not agree in their commentary on these words of St. Paul. The majority, following St. John Chrysostom, Theodoret, and

---

1 Cf. *Biblia Sacra iuxta Vulgatæ exemplaria et correctoria Romana* (Paris, 1887), III Reg. XII, 32-33: "Constituitque diem solemnem in mense octavo, quintadecima die mensis, in similitudinem solemnitatis quæ celebrabatur in Iuda. Et ascendens altare, similiter fecit in Bethel, ut immolaret vitulis quos fabricatus fuerat; constituitque in Bethel sacerdotes excelsorum quæ fecerat. Et ascendit super altare quod exstruxerat in Bethel, . . . quem finxerat de corde suo; et fecit solemnitatem filiis Israel, et ascendit super altare ut adoleret incensum." So also in IV Reg. XXIII, 12, 15-16; XVI, 10-12; II Paral. XIV, 2; XXXIII, 15-16; both names are used side by side for altars to false gods in IV Reg. XXI, 4-5: "Exstruxitque aras in domo Domini, de qua dixit Dominus: In Ierusalem ponam nomen meum. Et exstruxit altaria universæ militiæ cæli in duobus atriis templi Domini."

2 Cf. *Biblia Sacra,* Num. XXIII, 1-2, 4, 29-30; Ecclus. L, 13, 15; Baruch I, 10: "Offerte pro peccato ad aram Dei nostri."

3 Cf. *Biblia Sacra,* Act. XVII, 23: "Præteriens enim, et videns simulacra vestra, inveni et aram in qua scriptum erat: Ignoto Deo."

others [4] maintain it refers to the altar as the place of sacrifice; while a few, in accordance with the explanation of St. Thomas Aquinas [5], claim it refers, not to the Eucharist and the Eucharistic sacrifice, but to Christ and the cross of Christ.[6]

In the Old Testament *mensa* is used for the table of the loaves of proposition; but there are a few instances in which it signifies the altar.[7] In the New Testament St. Paul uses *mensa* to represent the Eucharistic table.[8] Although the Apostle in this text does not formally declare that the Eucharistic table here means the table of sacrifice, i. e., the altar, the Council of Trent states that from the context of the words of the Apostle *mensa* clearly indicates the altar.[9]

In the Septuagint and Greek text of the New Testament the distinction between θυσιαστήριον and βωμός is not as pronounced as between *altare* and *ara* in the Vulgate. Moreover, βωμός is but seldom used to designate altar, the usual Greek term being θυσιαστήριον.[10]

§ 2. *Terms used by the Romans and Greeks.*

The usual word with the Romans for designating the altar was *ara; altare* was seldom used. Roman scholars and grammarians attempt to distinguish between *ara* and *altare,* but if an examination is made of the texts quoted by Festus and Servius to prove the difference, it will be found that the terms are synonymous. Vergil uses both terms interchangeably.[11] It is interesting to note that in the classical period the word *altare* is used only in the plural to indicate one or more altars. The singular form is not found until the time of

---

4 Gattico, *De Usu Altaris Portatilis,* cap. 1, n. 4; Bona, *Rerum Liturgicarum,* lib. I, cap. 20, n. 1.

5 "Istud altare vel est crux Christi, in qua Christus immolatus est, vel ipse Christus, in quo et per quem preces nostras offerimus."—*Commentarium in Epistolam ad Hebræos,* cap. 13, lectio II, *Opera Omnia,* XXI, 728 f.

6 Cf. Benedict XIV, *De Sacrificio Missæ,* lib. I, cap. 2, n. 3; Braun, *Der christliche Altar,* I, 21.

7 Cf. Ezek. XLI, 22; XLIV, 16; Mal. I, 7, 12.

8 I Cor. X, 21.

9 "Et hæc quidem illa munda oblatio est . . .; et quam non obscure innuit apostolus Paulus Corinthiis scribens, cum dicit: Non posse eos, qui participatione mensæ dæmoniorum polluti sint, mensæ Domini participes fieri: per mensam altare utrobique intelligens."—Sess. XXII, *de Sacrificio Missæ,* c. 1.

10 Braun, *op. cit.,* I, 22; Kraus, *Real-Encyklopädie der christlichen Alterthümer,* I, 34.

11 Cf. *Thesaurus Linguæ Latinæ* (Leipsic, 1900—), s. v. *altare,* I, 1725 ff.; s. v. *ara,* II, 382 f.

Petronius (d. cir. 66), and even after his time it was rarely used in the singular by pagan authors. On the contrary the singular form *altare* was more frequently used by the Christian writers, until later it finally replaced the plural entirely.[12]

Mensæ, "tables," were used by the Romans in the temples as places where they laid the vessels used in the sacrifices, or they were used for such offerings as were not to be burnt, but to be consecrated to the deity, as, for example, wine and fruits.[13]

Among the Greeks the regular term for altar was βωμός, although ἐσχάρα and τράπεζα are found occasionally.[14]

§ 3. *Terms Used by the Fathers and the Liturgical Documents.*

The words used by the Greek Fathers and liturgies to designate the Christian altar are τράπεζα and θυσιαστήριον. Βωμός, as contrasted with θυσιαστήριον, is used by the Greek Fathers for heathen altars. A few exceptions, however, are met with.[15] Clement of Alexandria [16] and Origen [17] also use the word βωμός, but in a figurative sense, when they say the soul of the faithful is the true Christian altar. In the passage just referred to in Origen, he expressly admits the charge of Celsus that Christians had no material altars. So also like expressions are found in Minucius Felix [18] and Arnobius.[19] The object of these writers was to distinguish between the pagan sacrifices and the unbloody Sacrifice of the New Law. In the pagan sense, it is true, Christians had neither temples nor altars.[20] It must be remembered also that the prevalence of the *Disciplina Arcani* during this period sufficiently accounts for the silence and caution on the part of ecclesiastical writers on this subject as well as other matters connected with Christian worship and the administration of the sacraments.

---

12 *Thesaurus Linguæ Latinæ, loc. cit.*

13 Daremberg-Saglio, *Dictionnaire des Antiquités Grecques et Romaines* (5 vols., Paris, 1877-1919), s. v. *mensa,* III (part 2), 1720.

14 Kraus, *Real-Encyklopädie der christlichen Alterthümer,* I, 34.

15 Cf. Synesius, *Catastasis,* Migne, *P. G.,* LXVI, 1573.

16 *Stromatum,* lib. VII, cap. 6, Migne, *P. G.,* IX, 444.

17 *Contra Celsum,* lib. VIII, cap. 17, Migne, *P. G.,* XI, 1541.

18 "Cur nullas aras habent, templa nulla, nulla nota simulacra?"—*Octavius,* cap. 10, *Corpus Scriptorum Eccles. Latin.,* II, 14.

19 *Adversus Nationes,* lib. VI, n. 1, *Corpus Scriptorum Eccles. Latin.,* IV, 214.

20 Benedict XIV, *De Sacrificio Missæ,* lib. I, cap. 2, n. 2; Schuster, *The Sacramentary,* I, 142.

Τράπεζα, when it refers to the Eucharistic table, is very often modified by epithets expressive of awe and reverence, as ἱερά [21], ἁγία [22], μυστική [23], and the like; sometimes it stands alone, when the meaning is evident from the context; then again it is called τράπεζα Κυρίου, *mensa Domini*, "table of the Lord" [24], as occurs in St. Paul's epistle, I Cor. X, 21. Θυσιαστήριον and τράπεζα, however, do not designate different objects, but are different names for the place of the Eucharistic sacrifice. Both terms continued to be used by the Greeks to designate the altar, although τράπεζα came more in favor and is the usual term in the Greek liturgies.

The term usually employed from the very beginning by the Latin Fathers and Western liturgical documents to designate the altar is *altare*. Thus its use is found in Tertullian [25], St. Cyprian [26], St. Ambrose [27], St. Optatus, bishop of Milevis [28], St. Augustine [29], and other Latin Fathers. *Ara*, the Vulgate rendering of βωμός, is not applied to the Christian altar by any early ecclesiastical writer except Tertullian, who uses the phrase *ara Dei*.[30] The use of *ara* was usually avoided on account of its pagan associations. When Christianity had made much progress and the danger of association with pagan customs and practices had passed, the Fathers sometimes made use of *ara* to designate the altar. Its use in the sense of the Christian altar may be found in the sermon of St. Augustine on St. Stephen [31],

---

21 St John Chrysostom, *Contra Iudæos et Gentiles*, nn. 8, 9, Migne, *P. G.*, XLVIII, 824, 826; Synesius, *Catastasis*, Migne, *P. G.*, LXVI, 1569; Socrates, *Historia Ecclesiastica*, lib. I, cap. 37, Migne, *P. G.*, LXVII, 176; Sozomen, *Historia Ecclesiastica*, lib. V, cap. 20, lib. VIII, cap. 7, lib. IX, cap. 1, Migne, *P. G.*, LXVII, 1280, 1533, 1596.

22 St. Gregory of Nyssa, *In Baptismum Christi, Oratio in diem Luminum*, Migne, *P. G.*, XLVI, 581.

23 St. Gregory Nazianzen, *Carmina*, lib. II, sect. 1, n. 11, v. 1884, Migne, *P. G.*, XXXVII, 1161; St. John Chrysostom, *De Pœnitentia Homilia IX*, Migne, *P. G.*, XLIX, 345.

24 Origen, *Contra Celsum*, lib. VIII, cap. 24, Migne, *P. G.*, XI, 1553.

25 *De Ieiunio adversus psychicos*, cap. 16, *Corpus Scriptorum Eccles. Latin.*, XX, 295-296.

26 *Epistula LXV*, cap. 2, 3, *Corpus Scriptorum Eccles. Latin.*, III (part 2), 723, 724.

27 *Exhortatio Virginitatis*, cap, 2, n. 10, cap. 14, n. 94, Migne, *P. L.*, XVI, 339, 364; *Epistola XXII*, n. 13, Migne, *P. L.*, XVI, 1023.

28 *De Schismate Donatistarum*, lib. VI, cap. 1, 2, Migne, *P. L.*, XI, 1064, 1065.

29 *Sermo 90*, n. 5, Migne, *P. L.*, XXXVIII, 562; *Confessiones*, lib. IX, cap. 13, n. 36, *Corpus Scriptorum Eccles. Latin.*, XXXIII, 225; and in many other places of his works.

30 *De Oratione*, cap. 19, *Corpus Scriptorum Eccles. Latin.*, XX, 192.

31 *Sermo 318*, n. 1, Migne, *P. L.*, XXXVIII, 1438.

in the sermon of St. Maximus of Turin on St. Cyprian [32], in the *Codex Theodosianus* [33], and in St. Ambrose.[34] Prudentius uses *ara* as the designation of the base of the altar: *"Altaris aram funditus pessumdare."*[35] By the later writers *ara* is rarely used, and, when used, came to mean usually the table part of the altar. In the second half of the Middle Ages, *ara* is used for portable altar *(altare portatile),* principally in Spain.[36] When the Roman Missal was published in 1570, *ara* was incorporated in the general rubrics in the sense of portable altar [37], and ever since has had this exclusive signification.[38] With this meaning is the term *ara* employed in the Code of Canon Law.[39]

Mensa was employed to some extent to designate the altar by the Latin Fathers, but not nearly as much as τράπεζα had been used by the Greek Fathers. By later writers the word *mensa* came to be used exclusively for the top of the altar as distinguished from the support *(stipes)* which propped the table. After this distinction came to be made, *altare* is rarely used to designate the table part of the altar.

The plural *altaria* is sometimes used with the significance of a singular.[40] The singular form, *altarium,* in its different forms for case construction, is used sometimes by writers for *altare.*[41] *Altarium* is also used as a designation of the free space about the altar.[42]

In the West, especially since the Renaissance, *altare* came to mean the whole structure—support, table, reredos—as regards the fixed altar, and became applicable in a broad sense also to the altar-stone, upon which Mass is said when a fixed altar cannot be had.

---

32 *Sermo 78,* Migne, *P. L.,* LVII, 689.

33 "Confugientibus aram salutis esse præcipimus."—L. 9, art. 45, n. 4.

34 *De Virginibus,* lib. I, cap. 2, n. 65, Migne, *P. L.,* XVI, 206.

35 *Peristephanon,* Hymn. X, v. 49, Migne, *P. L.,* LX, 448.

36 Braun, *Der christliche Altar,* I, 33.

37 Missale Rom., *Rubricæ generales missalis,* c. XX, *de præparatione altaris, et ornamentorum eius.*

38 Corblet, *Histoire du Sacrement de l'Eucharistie,* II, 65.

39 Cf. Can. 1197, § 1, n. 2; can. 1199, §§ 1, 2; can. 239, § 1, n. 7.

40 St. Ambrose, *Epistola* XX, n. 8, Migne, *P. L.,* XVI, 997; St. Paulinus of Nola, *Epistola XXXII,* cap. 6, 8, 17, *Corpus Scriptorum Eccles. Latin.,* XXIX, 281, 283, 292; *Codex Theodosianus,* L. 9, art. 45, n. 4.

41 Cf., for example, St. Augustine, *Epistola 54 ad Inquisitiones Ianuarii,* cap. 3, Migne, *P. L.,* XXXIII, 201; St. Ambrose, *In I. Cor.,* cap. 9, Migne, *P. L.,* XVII, 230.

42 St. Gregory of Tours in his *Historia Francorum,* lib. II, cap. 14, speaks of a church having *fenestras in altario triginta duas.*—*Monumenta Germaniæ Historica, Scriptores Rerum Merovingicarum,* I, 82.

Thus today the component parts of a fixed altar are the *mensa* (table), the *stipes* (support), and the *sepulcrum* (sepulchre or cavity for the relics), whereas for the *altare portatile* (portable altar) it is required only that it be a stone sufficiently large to hold the chalice and sacred host in the celebration of Holy Mass.

§ 4. *Etymology of altare and ara.*

Many explanations are given as to the etymology of *altare* and *ara* by grammarians and philologists. Festus, the Roman grammarian, gives three classifications: *a*) *altare* is from *adolescere*, "to burn or to be kindled," because on it the flames rose up; *b*) from *adolere*, "to burn or consume by fire," because on the altar the offering was burnt up or consumed; *c*) from *altus, altitudo*, because the *altaria* consecrated to the higher deities show a construction rising up from the earth, being built up high.[43] The older grammarians and commentators give only this last explanation. An old Latin glossary declares that *altare* is derived from the two words, *alta* and *res*, because on the altar there is consummated *alta res, id est divina;* although another glossary gives the explanation that *altare* comes from *altitudo*.[44] Isidore of Seville gives the latter derivation: *"Altare autem ab altitudine constat esse nominatum quasi alta ara."*[45] Honorius of Autun[46] and Sicardus of Cremona[47] accept both explanations as found in the glossary.

Modern philologists do not agree on the etymology of *altare*. Some deduce it from *altus*[48], although the latest and perhaps preferable opinion, expressed by A. Walde[49], is that *altare* is derived from *adoleo*, "to burn a sacrifice." The fact mentioned before that the

---

43 Festus, *De Verborum Significatu quæ supersunt cum Pauli Epitome* (Budapest, 1889): p. 4, "Adolescit a græco ἀλδήσκω id est adcresco venit, unde fiunt . . . . . altare, eo quod in illo ignis excrescit. . . . . . Altaria sunt, in quibus igne adoletur." P. 21, "Altaria ab altitudine sunt dicta, quod antiqui diis superis in ædificiis a terra exaltatis sacra faciebant; diis terrestribus in terra, diis infernalibus in effossa terra."

44 *Corpus Glossariorum Latinorum* (7 vols., Leipsic, 1888-1901), V, 424, l. 3; V, 438, l. 54.

45 *Etymologiarum*, lib. IV, cap. 4, n. 14, Migne, *P. L.*, LXXXII, 545.

46 *Gemma Animæ*, lib. I, cap. 122, Migne, *P. L.*, CLXXII, 584.

47 *Mitrale*, lib. I, cap. 3, Migne, *P. L.*, CCXIII, 18.

48 *Thesaurus Linguæ Latinæ*, I, 1725; R. A. S. Macalister, in the *Encyclopedia Britannica* (11. ed.), s. v. *altar*, I, 759.

49 *Lateinisches Etymologisches Wörterbuch* (2. ed., Heidelberg, 1910), p. 28; he states that "Verbindung mit *altus* ist farblos."

word was originally used in the plural would seem to favor the explanation that *altare* comes from *alta ara;* the meaning of *altaria* then would be that which goes to make up the height, the height being either the elevation of the altar, or the upper part of the altar, or the offering laid on the altar.[50] Canonists and liturgists of recent years seem to favor the opinion that *altare* is derived from *alta ara*.[51]

The same disagreement among authors is noticeable in the derivation of *ara.* Some authors, after Varro[52], derive *ara* from *area;* others, following Servius[53], obtain it from the Greek word ἀρά *(precatio).* Isidore of Seville has the following explanation: *"Aram quidam vocatam dixerunt, quod ibi incensæ victimæ ardebant, alii aras dicant a precationibus, i. e. quas Græci ἀράς vocant."*[54] So also Honorius of Autun[55] and Sicardus of Cremona.[56] Modern philologists derive *ara* from *areo,* "burn."[57]

---

50 Braun, *Der christliche Altar,* I, 24.

51 Gasparri, *De SS. Eucharistia,* I, n. 281; Corblet, *Histoire du Sacrement de l'Eucharistie,* II, 65; Rock, *Hierurgia,* II, 293, footnote 2; Van der Stappen, *Sacra Liturgia,* III, 12; Gihr, *The Holy Sacrifice of the Mass,* p. 236, footnote 3; Ferraris, *Bibliotheca,* s. v. *altare,* I, 213; Rohault de Fleury, *La Messe,* I, 93; Thalhofer, *Handbuch der katholischen Liturgik,* I, 748; Wapelhorst, *Compendium Sacræ Liturgiæ,* p. 13, footnote; Cappello, *De Sacramentis,* I, 617; Bargilliat, *Prælectiones Iuris Canonici,* II, n. 1430; Fanfani, *De Iure Parochorum,* p. 31; Cocchi, *Commentar. in Codicem Iuris Canonici, lib. III, pars II et III, De Locis et Temporibus Sacris,* p. 24.

52 *De Lingua Latina* (Berlin, 1826), p. 39.

53 *Commentarium in Vergilii Aeneidos Libros,* II, 515.

54 *Etymologiarum,* lib. XV, cap. 4, n. 13, Migne, *P. L.,* LXXXII, 545.

55 *Gemma Animæ,* lib. I, cap. 122, Migne, *P. L.,* CLXXII, 584.

56 *Mitrale,* lib. I, cap. 3, Migne, *P. L.,* CCXIII, 18.

57 Cf. *Thesaurus Linguæ Latinæ,* II, 328; Walde, *Lateinisches Etymologisches Wörterbuch,* p. 54.

CHAPTER III

VARIOUS KINDS OF ALTARS

The altar in the strict sense of the liturgy consists of a plane stone table, rectangular or square, fixed or movable, consecrated for the offering of the Holy Sacrifice of the Mass. In the usual acceptation of the word, adopted in the rubrics themselves, the name of altar is given to the table that rests upon the foundation, and also to the support of the table itself. According to the liturgical acceptation, the use and location in a church, the following distinctions are made in regard to altars upon which Holy Mass may be celebrated.

1. In accordance with the manner of construction and consecration, in the strict liturgical sense, an altar is either fixed *(altare fixum seu immobile)* or portable *(altare portatile seu mobile, ara portatilis, petra sacra)*.

a) A fixed or immovable altar is a permanent structure of stone, consisting of the table *(mensa)* upon which the Holy Sacrifice is offered and the support or base *(stipes)* consecrated together as one whole.[1]

b) A portable or movable altar consists of a solid piece of natural stone, generally of small size, which alone is consecrated; or the same stone with its support, which, however, was not consecrated together with the table as one whole.[2]

c) Midway between the fixed and portable altars is another type of altar quite prevalent in churches which may be called quasi-fixed, or in the words of the Sacred Congregation of Rites *ad modum fixi*.[3] This altar is a permanent structure of wood, cement, or any other suitable and becoming material or composition, in which a consecrated altar-stone is inserted. In the strict liturgical sense these structures enjoy the character only of portable altars. They have the advantage,

[1] "Sensu liturgico intelligitur nomine altaris immobilis seu fixi, mensa superior una cum stipitibus per modum unius cum eadem consecratis."—Can. 1197, § 1, n. 1.

[2] "Sensu liturgico intelligitur nomine altaris mobilis seu portatilis, petra, ut plurimum, parva, quæ sola consecratur, quæque dicitur etiam ara portatilis seu petra sacra; vel eadem petra cum stipite qui tamen non fuit una cum eadem consecratus."—Can. 1197, § 1, n. 2.

[3] 31 Aug. 1867, ad 1, *Decr. Auth.*, n. 3162.

however, of being made privileged altars[4] and of receiving the title of a saint[5], which portable altars in themselves do not possess.

The fixed altar is the altar in the truest sense of the word and is the normal altar for the church, so that in every consecrated church there must be at least one fixed altar.[6] The portable altar supplies the place of the fixed altar in the church, when from a variety of circumstances the fixed altar cannot always be built. The Church sanctions this practice, and has laid down rules in her liturgy and code of laws regulating the construction and use of such altars.[7]

2. By reason of excellence and location, altars may be *a*) privileged, *b*) papal, *c*) high or side altars.

a) A privileged altar is one to which is attached a special indulgence by way of suffrage for the souls in purgatory whenever holy Mass is celebrated upon it.[8] The privilege consists in this that in addition to the ordinary fruits of the Eucharistic sacrifice a plenary indulgence, applicable to the individual soul for which the Mass is offered, may be gained whenever Mass is said thereon. This privilege is granted only to fixed altars, but in this sense is included also the quasi-fixed altar or altar *ad modum fixi*.[9]

b) A papal altar is so called either because it was consecrated by the Pope or because he said Mass upon it or because he has directly granted this special distinction to it.[10] On papal altars no one, not even a Cardinal or a bishop, may say Mass without an apostolic indult.[11] Examples of papal altars are the high altars of the patriarchal basilicas in Rome of St. John Lateran, St. Peter, St. Paul, and Santa Maria Maggiore.

---

4 S. R. C., 31 Aug. 1867, ad 1, *Decr. Auth.*, n. 3162.

5 "Sicut ecclesia, ita quodlibet etiam ecclesiæ altare, saltem immobile, proprium sibi titulum habeat. Titulus primarius altaris maioris idem debet esse ac titulus ecclesiæ."—Can. 1201, §§ 1-2.

6 "In ecclesia consecrata saltem unum altare, præsertim maius, debet esse immobile."—Can. 1197, § 2.

7 Can. 1197, § 2; can. 1198, §§ 1, 3, 4; can. 1199, § 1; can. 1201, §§ 1-3; can. 1202, § 1.

8 There are also altars which are privileged for the living, or for the living and the dead; but such altars are an exception today and are seldom found outside of Rome. The nature of these altars will be considered under the special chapter devoted to the privileged altar in Part III.

9 S. R. C., 31 Aug. 1867, ad 1, *Decr. Auth.*, n. 3162; cf. Van der Stappen, *Sacra Liturgia*, III, 16; Many, *Prælectiones de Locis Sacris*, pp. 223-225.

10 Cf. Benedict XIV, ep. *Dilectus Filius*, 15 Ian. 1745, § 1, *Fontes I. C.*, n. 352; Augustine, *A Commentary*, IV, 174 f.

11 "In altaribus papalibus nemo celebret sine apostolico indulto."—Can. 823, § 3.

c) The high altar *(altare maius)* is the one that occupies the principal place of honor in the church.[12] All other altars in a church are called side altars *(altaria minora vel secundaria)*. This distinction between high and side altars arose when many altars were introduced in the churches, and is used in those churches having more than one altar to distinguish the main altar from the other altars in the church.[13]

3. The distinctions given above are the principal divisions of the altar as it is found in the Western Church today. Besides these, in the study of the Christian altar and in many churches of Europe and other continents, the following varieties of altars are found:

a) Matutinal altar, found usually in monastic churches, is an altar situated in the choir for the celebration of Mass immediately following matins. Another name very similar to this was the *altare de retro,* where the early morning Mass was celebrated for pilgrims. It is so called, because it was usually found in the apse behind the high altar.[14]

b) Altar of the dead, an altar upon which the funeral Masses were celebrated.[15]

c) Altar of the Blessed Sacrament, so called because the Holy Eucharist is kept in the tabernacle built in connection with the altar.

d) Gregorian altar is the name given to the altar of St. Gregory in the church of the same name on the Cælian Hill in Rome. The Gregorian altar *ad instar* is given to those altars which through a concession of the Roman Pontiff share in the privileges of the altar of the Church of St. Gregory on the Cælian Hill.[16] These altars are the equivalent of a privileged altar.[17]

e) Altar of the Holy Cross, an altar occupying a very prominent place in the cathedral, monastic, and religious churches of the Middle Ages in the different European countries. Many of these altars are still extant. The altar of the Holy Cross stood usually in the middle

12 Many names have been given to the high altar in the course of time, especially in the Middle Ages. The most important of these are: *altare authenticum, capitaneum, titulariorum, cardinale, dominicale vel dominicum, magistrum, princeps vel principale, primum, summum, senius.* Cf. Braun, *Der christliche Altar,* I, 34-37.

13 Coronata, *De Locis et Temporibus Sacris,* p. 102.

14 Rock, *The Church of our Fathers,* I, 177; Braun, *op. cit.,* I, 36.

15 Corblet, *Histoire du Sacrement de l'Eucharistie,* II, 64.

16 Cf. *Ephemerides Liturgicæ,* XXX (1916), 362-363.

17 S. C. S. Off. (Sect. de Indulg.), 12 Dec. 1912, *Acta Apost. Sedis,* V (1913), 33.

of the church or of the nave of the church; in the churches having a choir, it stood often between the choir and body of the church. In the period following the Middle Ages, the altar of the Holy Cross was gradually removed from its place of honor. Behind the altar of the Holy Cross was a large crucifix, preferably erected on a pillar. A crucifix in the middle of the church was really significant and beautiful; dominating the whole interior and within sight of all, it announced to him who entered the character of the church, and told him that in this church Christ the crucified was Lord and King, that in it the God-Man renewed in an unbloody manner the sacrifice of Golgatha and that for mankind salvation and eternal life are to be found only in the cross.[18]

4. In the churches of the Greek rite, only one altar is erected upon which only one Mass may be celebrated in the same day. In this practice the Greeks together with most of the Orientals have preserved the ancient custom of having only one altar in their churches, upon which they celebrated only once a day. However, to satisfy the wishes of those who desire to celebrate privately, the Greeks erect small chapels or oratories near the principal church or adjoining the walls of the church. One altar is constructed in each chapel, in which a Greek priest carries out the liturgy privately once a day. These chapels or oratories are called *parecclesiæ,* as it were, additions to the church. Moreover, at the present time besides their own altar the Greeks often erect a Latin altar in their churches for the use of the Latin priests.[19]

For a portable altar in the Greek rite, the *antimension* is used. It consists of a strip of fine linen or silk, usually ten inches wide and about thirteen to fourteen inches long, ornamented with the instruments of the Passion, or with a representation of our Lord in the sepulchre; it also contains relics of the saints which are sewn into it, and certified by the bishop.[20] It is consecrated by the bishop, usually in connection with the consecration of a church, with as much cere-

---

18 Braun, *op. cit.,* I, 401-406.

19 Goar, *Euchologion sive Rituale Græcorum,* pp. 16, 28; cf. Benedict XIV, ep. encycl. *Demandatam,* 24 Dec. 1743, § 8, *Fontes I. C.,* n. 338; Gasparri, *De SS. Eucharistia,* I, n. 287; *American Ecclesiastical Review,* III (1890), 91-93; Renaudot, *Liturgiarum Orientalium Collectio,* I, 165; Zitelli-Solieri, *Apparatus Iuris Ecclesiastici,* n. 1174.

20 *American Ecclesiastical Review,* III (1890), 90-91; *Catholic Encyclopedia,* I, 563 f.; Zitelli-Solieri, *op. cit.,* n. 1173; Braun, *Der christliche Altar,* I, 519 ff.

mony and solemnity as the portable altar of the Latin Church. The *antimension* is required to be placed on the altar in Greek churches just as an altar-stone is required in the Latin churches, and no Mass may be said upon an altar of the Greek rite which has no *antimension*. However, by special regulation of the Holy See, the United Greeks in the absence of the *antimension* may celebrate Mass upon a consecrated altar-stone. Originally it was intended for missionaries and priests travelling in places where there was no consecrated altar, or where there was no bishop available to consecrate an altar. Although a Latin priest may celebrate Mass on a consecrated altar of any Catholic rite in the absence of an altar of his own rite, he may not celebrate Mass upon the *antimension* of the Greeks without a special indult from the Apostolic See.[21]

---

21 "Deficiente altari proprii ritus, sacerdoti fas est ritu proprio celebrare in altari consecrato alius ritus catholici, non autem super Græcorum *antimensiis*."—Can. 823, § 2.

SECTION 2

THE HISTORY OF THE LEGISLATION CONCERNING ALTARS

CHAPTER I

THE MATERIAL OF ALTARS

§ 1. *Wood and Stone as Material*

It is generally admitted by all authors that the material of the earliest altars was more generally, though not always, wood.[1] No ducumentary evidence for the first three centuries is extant, nor have any altars of this period been preserved to posterity. At Rome, however, a wooden table is still preserved in the Lateran Basilica, and fragments of another such table are preserved in the church of St. Pudentiana, on which St. Peter is said to have celebrated Mass. Although no certain proofs can be put forward to uphold these statements [2], nevertheless it is of importance that these altars are of wood, thereby indicating the traditional belief that the earliest altars were of that material.

Abundant proof is at hand to show that in Northern Africa the altars were usually made of wood to the end of the fourth century. St. Optatus, bishop of Milevis, describing the violence of the Donatists, mentions their planing afresh, or breaking up and using for firewood, the altars in the churches of their rivals.[3] St. Augustine

---

1 Benedict XIV, *De Sacrificio Missæ,* lib. I, cap. 2, n. 5; Martène, *De Antiquis Ecclesiæ Ritibus,* lib. I, cap. 3, art. 6, n. 2; Bona, *Rerum Liturgicarum,* lib. I, cap. 20, n. 1; Thalhofer, *Handbuch der katholischen Liturgik,* I, 754; Rock, *Hierurgia,* II, 300; O'Brien, *History of the Mass,* p. 113; Hedley, *The Holy Eucharist,* p. 211; Gattico, *De Usu Altaris Portatilis,* cap. 2, n. 1; Braun, *Der christliche Altar,* I, 101 ff.

2 Cabrol, *Dictionnaire d'Archéologie Chrétienne et de Liturgie,* I, (part 2), 3158; Braun, *op. cit.,* I, 56-58.

3 "Alio loco copia lignorum frangi (altaria), aliis vero ut altaria raderent, lignorum inopia imperavit. .... Quid perditorum conductam referam multitudinem et vinum in mercedem sceleris datum, quod ut immundo ore sacrilegis haustibus biberetur, calida de fragmentis altarium facta est."—*De Schismate Donatistarum,* lib. VI, n. 1, Migne, *P.L.,* XI, 1063 ff.

declares that the Donatists beat the Catholic Bishop Maximianus with the wood of the altar under which he had taken refuge.[4] So also in the East, mention is made of altars of wood. Thus St. Athanasius, in speaking of an outrage perpetrated by the Arians, enumerates, amongst other articles of church furniture which they had burned, the sacred table, which was of wood.[5] It was not until after a considerable period that wooden altars were altogether superseded by those of stone. Pope St. Silvester (314-335) is said to have been the first to make stone altars obligatory,[6] but this statement has no convincing proof, both because the decree is not found among the acts attributed to this pope, many of which are extant,[7] and because wooden altars existed and were used after his time.[8]

The first actual legislation against wooden altars, that is known, dates from the Council of Epaon, in Gaul, in 517, which forbade the consecration of any but stone altars.[9] As this council was only provincial, this prohibition concerned only a small part of the Christian world, and for several centuries afterward altars of stone were used. The fourteenth chapter of the Capitularies of Charlemagne, in 769, orders that priests should not celebrate Mass unless *"in mensis lapideis ab Episcopis consecratis."*[10] And in a capitulary of 806, Charlemagne merely renewed the legislation of the Council of Epaon, only a fragment of which has been left to us.[11] This seems to mark a period when the use of wooden altars, although disapproved of, was by no means unknown. In England William of Malmesbury relates that St. Wulstan, bishop of Worcester (1062-1095), demolished the wooden altars which still remained in his

---

4 *Epistola 185*, cap. 7, n. 27, Migne, *P.L.*, XXXIII, 805.

5 *Historia Arianorum ad Monachos*, cap. 56, Migne, *P.G.*, XXV, 760.

6 "Constantinus imperator.....ecclesiam ædificavit. Quam Sanctus Silvester Papa ... consecraverat, dedicavit, et in ea altare lapideum, chrismate delibutum, erexit; atque ex eo tempore sancivit ne deinceps altaria nisi ex lapide fierent."—*Breviarium Romanum, In Dedicatione Bas. SS. Petri et Pauli App.*, 18 Nov., lectio V.

7 *Liber Pontificalis*, I, 170-187.

8 Cf. Benedict XIV, *De Sacrificio Missæ*, lib. I, cap. 2, n. 6; Bona, *Rerum Liturgicarum*, lib. I, cap. 20, n. 1.

9 Can. 26: "Altaria nisi lapidea chrismatis unctione non sacrentur."—*Monumenta Germaniæ Historica, Legum Sectio III, Concilia*, I, 25. Cf. Hefele, Conciliengeschichte, II, 684.

10 *Monumenta Germaniæ Historica, Legum Sectio II, Capitularia Regum Francorum*, I, 46.

11 N. 16: "De Altaria non consecranda nisi lapidea."—*Monumenta Germaniae Historica, Legum Sectio II, Capitularia Regum Francorum*, I, 133.

diocese as in ancient times.[12] Martène [13] and Mabillon [14] have shown that wooden altars were used in Gaul in the first centuries of the Christian era. So were they also used in Spain, for the Council of Coyaca, in 1050, deemed it necessary to prescribe that the altar must be of stone.[15] The Synod of Winchester in England prescribed the same in 1076.[16]

It is certain that from a very early date stone altars were in use, especially in those places where the persecutions were not raging in which fixed altars could be set up, and it is scarcely to be doubted that there is a close conection between them and the tombs of martyrs. St. Gregory Thaumaturgus in the third century built a vast basilica in Neo-Cæsarea in which it is probable that quite substantial altars were erected, for a short while later St. Gregory of Nyssa and St. John Chrysostom speak of stone as being the usual material of the altar. Thus St. Gregory of Nyssa mentions the consecration of an altar made of stone.[17] In a similar manner St. John Chrysostom writes of stone as the material of the altar.[18]

The testimony given above for the sixth and following centuries is sufficient to prove that the practice had become general in the West to erect altars only of stone. Thus in a letter of Pope St. Nicholas I to the Emperor Michael in 869, it is stated that the altar is of stone, differing not at all from other stones which are found in the walls and pavements; it is made sacred, however, by the help of God and the blessing which it receives, whereby it becomes a holy table.[19] This indicates that it had become the practice at Rome to have the altar constructed only of stone.

---

12 "Erant tunc temporis altaria lignea iam inde a priscis diebus in Anglia. Ea ille per diœcesim demolitus, ex lapidibus compaginavit alia."—*De Vita S. Wulstani,* lib. III, cap. 14, Migne, *P.L.,* CLXXIX, 1763.

13 *De Antiquis Ecclesiæ Ritibus,* lib. I, cap. 3, art. 6, n. 5.

14 *Acta SS. Benedict.,* Sæc. VI, pars II, p. 860.

15 Can. 3: "Altaris vero ara tota fit lapidea et ab Episcopis consecrata."—Hardouin, *Acta Conciliorum,* VI, 1026. Also in Mansi, *Conciliorum Collectio,* XIX, 786; Hefele, *Conciliengeschichte,* IV, 756.

16 Can. 5: "De Altaribus, ut lapidea sint."—Hardouin, *Acta Conciliorum,* VI, 1560.

17 *In Baptismum Christi, Oratio in diem Luminum,* Migne, *P.G.,* XLVI, 581.

18 *Commentarium in Epist. II ad Cor.,* Homilia XX, Migne, *P.G.,* LXI, 540; *Commentarium in Ioannem,* Homilia LXXIII, n. 3, Migne, *P.G.,* LIX, 399.

19 "Altare itaque sanctum, in quo Deo omnipotenti sacrificiorum vota persolvimus, lapis est naturaliter communis, nihil differens ab aliis tabulis, quae parietes nostros et pavimenta adornant. Quia vero sacratum est Dei adiutorio, et benedictionem suscepit, unde mensa sancta efficitur."—

§ 2. *Metal as Material*

Altars of precious metals were also in use in the period preceding the time, when stone became the established rule. Sixtus III gave an altar of purest silver weighing three hundred pounds to the Liberian Basilica, now Santa Maria Maggiore.[20] *Breviarius de Hierosolyma* in describing Jerusalem mentions a gold and silver altar in the Church of the Holy Sepulchre erected over the place where the three crosses were found.[21] Pulcheria, sister of Theodosius II, presented an altar of gold to the church of St. Sophia, at Constantinople, in the early part of the fifth century.[22] In the next century a very full account is extant of the magnificent altar presented by Justinian to the new basilica of St. Sophia, constructed by him between the years 532 and 563.[23] Many references to metal altars occur in the *Liber Pontificalis*,[24] but it is not clear whether the altars mentioned were constructed of metal or of wood which was covered with metal.[25] Especially worthy of mention is the high altar of the Cathedral of St. Ambrose, Milan, probably erected before 835. It is 7 ft. 3 in. in length, 4 ft. 1 in. in height, and the *mensa* is 4 ft. 4 in. wide. The front is of gold, the back and sides of silver, and it is decorated with panels containing subjects in relief and with enamel work. It is probably the most elaborate specimen of its kind which has survived.[26]

Epistolæ et Decreta, IV, Ad Michaelem Imperatorem, Migne, *P. L.*, CXIX, 778; (Apud Mansi, *Conciliorum Collectio,* XV, 162-167; Hardouin, *Acta Conciliorum,* V, 125).

20 "Hic fecit basilicam sanctæ Mariæ, quae ab antiquis Liberii cognominabatur, iuxta macellum Libiæ, ubi et obtulit hoc: altarem argenteum purissimum, pens. lib. CCC."—*Liber Pontificalis,* I, 232.

21 "Est ibi desuper altare de argento et auro puro et novem columnæ, quæ sustinent illud altare et ipsa absida."—*Corpus Scriptorum Eccles. Latin.*, XXXIX, 153. Cf. Paulinus of Nola, *Epistola* XXXI, cap. 6, *Corpus Scriptorum Eccles. Latin.*, XXIX, 273.

22 "Denique et ea quæ decreverat amplius confirmaret, Deumque ac sacerdotes, et subditos omnes, testes haberet actorum suorum, ex auro et pretiosis lapidibus admirabile quoddam donarium operum quæ spectantur longe pulcherrimam, sacram mensam in ecclesia Constantinopolitana pro virginitate sua et pro fratris imperio dedicavit."—Sozomen, *Historia Ecclesiastica,* lib. IX, cap. 1, Migne, *P. G.*, LXVII, 1596.

23 *Pauli Silentiarii Descriptio S. Sophiæ,* Migne, *P.G.*, LXXXVI bis, 2148.

24 (Edit. Duchesne), I, 500; II, 18, 26, 33, 53, 113, 133.

25 Benedict XIV, *De Sacrificio Missæ,* lib. I, cap. 2, n. 8; Gattico, *De Usu Altaris Portatilis,* cap. 2, n. 3; Martène, *De Antiquis Ecclesiæ Ritibus,* lib. I. cap. 3, art. 6, n. 7.

26 Cabrol, *Dictionnarie d'Archéologie Chrétienne et de Liturgie,* fig. 1130; also I, 3171-3172.

§ 3. *Later Development and Legislation*

Since wood is subject to decay and the base metals to corrosion, while more precious metals are too expensive, stone became in course of time the ordinary material for an altar. The current of ecclesiastical legislation set steadily in favor of stone as the canonical material of the altar, and the rule was established that if not all, a part at least, must be of stone, sufficiently large for the sacred vessels to stand upon during the offering of the Holy Sacrifice of the Mass. A definite universal regulation concerning the material of the altar was not made in the Middle Ages. It is true that canon 26 of the Council of Epaon was taken into the collection of canonical laws of the Church as the *Decretum Gratiani*[27] and in the *Panormia* of Ivo of Chartres.[28] In accordance with these regulations canonists in their commentaries on the *Decretum Gratiani* argued that the altar must be of stone.[29] The final stage of this development is the general rubric of the Roman Missal, c. XX: "*Altare, in quo sacrosanctum Missæ sacrificium celebrandum est, debet esse lapideum, et ab Episcopo, sive ab Abbate facultatem a Sede Apostolica habente, consecratum; vel saltem ara lapidea, similiter ab Episcopo, vel Abbate, ut supra, consecrata, in eo inserta, quæ tam ampla sit, ut Hostiam et maiorem partem Calicis capiat.*" So also had this prescription passed into the Code of Canon Law, can. 1198, §§ 1-2: "*Tum mensa altaris immobilis tum petra sacra ex unico constent lapide naturali, integro et non friabili. In altari immobili tabula seu mensa lapidea ad integum altare protendi debet, et apte cum stipite cohærere; stipes autem sit lapideus vel saltem latera seu columellæ quibus mensa sustentatur sint ex lapide.*"

It was not so much the positive legislation of the Church, but rather the constantly spreading custom by which the regulation that altars were to be made of stone gradually became universal. Stone was used because it was found practically in all places; also added to this were its durability, strength, and symbolism. No other material, having these three properties, is so easily found and procured. Precious metals, while durable, are not so readily obtained. The signification of stone is in harmony with the symbolism of the altar.

---

27 C. 31, D. I, *de cons.*

28 Lib. II, cap. 32; cited here as can. 6, Conc. Hippon.; Migne, *P. L.*, CLXI, 1089.

29 Cf. Pasqualigo, *De Sacrificio Novæ Legis*, I, Q. 668, n. 2.

The stone as well as the altar represents Christ. The altar is a symbol of Christ according to a very old idea which can be traced back to the fourth century.[30] The symbolism according to which stone represents Christ is also biblical. St. Paul in writing to the Corinthians calls Christ the Rock whence all received the water of salvation.[31] Again in Holy Scripture Christ is called the stone that is rejected by the builders, but this same stone became the head of the corner and a stumbling block.[32]

Sicardus of Cremona[33] and Durandus[34] especially developed the symbolism of stone in order to show that the altar should be constructed of stone and the reason therefor. Liturgists and other writers of the late Middle Ages give another reason; namely, that the altar is the sepulchre, i. e., the tomb of Christ, so that it is only fit that the altar like the tomb should be made of stone.[35] In regard to the symbolic reason for stone as the material of the altar, it is well to recall the following words of Pasqualigo: "*Hæc autem est congruentia adinventa post factum; nam si statutum fuisset, quod altare esset ligneum, dici posset ita factum, quia significat Crucem, quæ fuit lignea; quia sicut Christus seipsum obtulit in Cruce, ita modo offertur in altari.*"[36]

---

30 Cf. Pseudo-Ambrosian work, *De Sacramentis,* lib. V, cap. 2, n. 7, Migne, *P.L.,* XVI, 447; Alcuin, *Commentarium in Apocal.,* lib. IV, cap. 6, v. 9, Migne, *P. L.,* C, 1126; Rupert, Abbas Tuitiensis, *De Divinis Officiis,* lib. V, cap. 30, Migne, *P.L.,* CLXX, 150; Honorius of Autun, *Gemma Animæ,* lib. III, cap. 86, Migne, *P. L.,* CLXXII, 665.

31 I Cor. X, 4.

32 Cf. Ps. CXVII, 22; Isa. XXVIII, 16; Matt. XXI, 42; Mark XII, 10; Luke XX, 17; I Pet. II, 7.

33 *Mitrale,* lib. I, cap. 3, Migne, *P. L.,* CCXIII, 18-19.

34 *Rationale Divinorum Officiorum,* lib. I, cap. 7, nn. 27 f.

35 St. Thomas Aquinas in his *Summa Theologica,* p. 3, Q. LXXXIII, art. III, is a typical example: "Quod quidem competit significatione huius sacramenti, tum quia altare significat Christum; dicitur autem I Corint., X, 4; Petra autem erat Christus; tum etiam quia corpus Christi in sepulcro lapideo fuit reconditum. Competit etiam quoad usum sacramenti. Lapis enim et solidus est, et de facile potest inveniri ubique, quod non erat necessarium in veteri lege, ubi fiebat in uno loco altare."

36 *De Sacrificio Novæ Legis,* I, Q. 668, n. 3.

CHAPTER II

THE FORM OF THE ALTAR

From the liturgical point of view the altar as constituted today can be distinguished by the table (*mensa*), the sepulchre or cavity for the holy relics (*sepulcrum*), and the support or base (*stipes*). It is especially according to the construction of the base that altars have differed one form the other in their logical and historical development.

Very little information concerning the form of the altar of the first centuries of the Church has been preserved, even less than that pertaining to the material of the altars; for the early Fathers, when making mention of the altar, usually treat of it in passing, while they are writing on some other topic usually in reference to the Holy Eucharist, and hence give us very little knowledge as to its actual composition or construction. Moreover, the form of the altar was not at all times the same in every locality. Altars of different construction are found not only in successive periods of time but also side by side in the particular periods.

As the earliest churches were, no doubt, ordinary dwelling houses adapted to the special requirements of Christian worship,[1] it is generally agreed among authors that the earliest altars were small tables of wood, round or square in shape, similar to those in use at the period for purposes of repast.[2] This view is supported by certain very early frescos which have survived, and which have as subject matter the consecration of the Holy Eucharist. The most ancient and remarkable of these frescos is known as *Fractio Panis,* found in the so-called *Capella Græca* in the catacomb of St. Priscilla, which dates from the first half of the second century. It represents seven persons seated on a semi-circular divan before a table of the same form. Another fresco, discovered in the cemetery of Calixtus,

1 Duchesne, *Christian Worship,* pp. 399 ff.; Martène, *De Antiqnis Ecclesiæ Ritibus,* lib. I, cap. 3, art. 5, n. 2.

2 Benedict XIV, *De Sacrificio Missæ,* lib. I, cap. 2, n. 5; Martène, *op. cit.,* lib. I, cap. 3, art. 6, nn. 2, 7; Gasparri, *De SS. Eucharistia,* I. n. 289; Many, *Prælectiones de Locis Sacris,* p. 195; Rohault de Fleury, *La Messe,* I, 100, and Plate XXII in appendix.

belongs to the latter half of the same century and represents a small three-legged table on which is seen a loaf and a fish and before which a person vested with the pallium stands and spreads his hands over those in prayer.[3] No doubt, at a comparatively early date, special tables were reserved for the celebration of Mass, and their form was distinguished from those in ordinary use; but for this period of transition no definite evidence can be produced.[4] These tables had to be such that they would not easily attract the attention of the persecutors. Even after the Peace of the Church and when stone was chosen as the material of the altar, the table form continued to be used until even late in the Middle Ages, usually having columns from one to five in number for the support of the table. Several table altars of stone, dating from the fifth century, have been preserved, at least in part.[5]

The persecutions, too, gave rise to celebrating Mass in the catacombs and, no doubt, this practice brought about a change in the form of the altar. Two types of altars are found in the catacombs: the *arcosolium* and the table altar.[6] The *arcosolium* was formed by cutting about three feet from the floor in the tufa wall of the wider spaces of the catacombs an ordinary loculus (opening) surmounted by an arch. In the wall below this opening an excavation was made sufficiently large to receive the bodies of one or more martyrs. A marble slab placed horizontally over the opening completed the tomb, which in this way became a kind of sarcophagus hewn out of the living rock. In the big halls of the catacombs which served as churches, the altar was detached from the walls and consisted of a quadrangular table resting on a pillar, or small columns, or on a structure of masonry in which were inclosed the relics of martyrs. These latter altars are considered as dating after the time of Constantine.[7] The celebration of the Eucharist, however, on the tombs of the martyrs or the *arcosolia* was, even in the first age, the excep-

3 Cf. Cabrol, *Dictionnaire d'Archéologie Chrétienne et de Liturgie*, I, fig. 172, fig. 1123; Schuster, *The Sacramentary*, I, 137; Lowrie, *Monuments of the Early Church*, pp. 224 ff.

4 Cabrol, *op. cit.*, I, 1123 f.

5 Lowrie, *op. cit.*, p. 160; Braun, *Der christliche Altar*, I, 125 ff.; Bishop, *On the History of the Christian Altar*, pp. 5, 21.

6 Corblet, *Histoire du Sacrement de l'Eucharistie*, II, 70 f.; De Rossi, *Roma Sotterranea*, III, 490 ff.

7 Corblet, *op. cit.*, II, 70; De Rossi, *op. cit.*, III, 491.

tion rather than the rule. There is no proof that the *arcosolia* were used regularly or even frequently for the Eucharistic sacrifice, whether for funerals or anniversaries of the martyrs.[8] On the other hand it cannot be claimed that the *arcosolia* were never used, for the celebration of the Eucharistic sacrifice in cemeteries was a custom of of great antiquity. It is expressly ordered in the *Apostolic Constitutions,* where the faithful are commanded to assemble in the cemeteries for the reading of Holy Scripture and recitation of psalms in honor of the martyrs and saints, and for the faithful departed; and also to offer the Eucharistic sacrifice in churches and cemeteries.[9] It is possible that the same custom is referred to as early as the year 155 in the *Letter to the Smyrneans* relating to the martyrdom of St. Polycarp. After mentioning that they have placed the relics of the martyr in a suitable place, they pray that they may be permitted to gather in that place, and to celebrate the anniversary of his martyrdom.[10] In the *Liber Pontificalis* it is stated of Pope Felix I (269-274): *"Hic constituit supra memorias martyrum missas celebrare."*[11] It seems, however, probable that this means only that he regulated an already existing practice, for in Asia Minor it appears to have been much older.[12] However this may be, it is clear from the testimony of the *Liber Pontificalis* that the custom referred to was regarded at the beginning of the sixth century as very ancient.[13] The intimate connection between altars and the relics of martyrs is shown by such passages as the words of the author of the treatise *De Aleatoribus,* who writes: *"Martyribus præsentibus supra mensam dominicam;"* [14] or of St. Augustine who thus writes of the altar erected on the site of the martyrdom of St. Cyprian: *"Mensa Deo constructa est; et tamen mensa dicitur Cypriani, non quia ibi est unquam Cypri-*

---

8 Braun, *Der christliche Altar,* I, 51-54.

9 "Sed absque ulla observatione vana, congregamini in cæmeteriis, ibique lectionem sacrorum librorum facite, et psallite super dormientibus martyribus et omnibus sanctis qui abierunt a sæculo; proque fratribus vestris qui in Domino dormierunt. Et antitypum regalis corporis Christi, ratam acceptamque eucharistiam offerte in ecclesiis et cæmeteriis vestris."—*Constitutiones Apostolicae,* lib. VI, n. 29 (*Didascalia XVII*), in Cardinal Pitra, *Iuris Ecclesiastici Græcorum Historia et Monumenta* (2 vols., Rome, 1864), I, 344.

10 Eusebius, *Historia Ecclesiastica,* lib. IV, cap. 15, Migne, *P.G.,* XX, 360.

11 (Edit. Duchesne), I, 158.

12 Schuster, *The Sacramentary,* I, 138.

13 (Edit. Duchesne), I, 158, note 2.

14 Cap. 11, *Corpus Scriptorum Eccles. Latin.,* III (part 3), 103.

anus epulatus, sed quia ibi est immolatus, et quia ipsa immolatione sua paravit hanc mensam, non in qua pascat sive pascatur, sed in qua sacrificium Deo, cui et ipse oblatus est, offeratur."[15] In this connection may also be quoted the famous lines of the poet Prudentius, who, speaking of St. Hippolytus, refers to the altar above his tomb, as follows:

Talibus Hippolyti corpus mandatur opertis
Propter ubi apposita est ara dicata Deo,
Illa sacramenti donatrix mensa eademque
Custos fida sui martyris adposita,
Servat ad æterni spem iudicis ossa sepulchro,
Pascit item sanctis tibricolas dapibus.[16]

With the age of peace, and especially under the pontificate of Pope Damasus (366-384), basilicas and chapels were erected in Rome and elsewhere. The change from the chapels in the catacombs or in private houses to these urban basilicas was quite easy. In them the fixed altar was erected rather than the blood-stained tomb of the martyr and constituted the center of the whole liturgical worship, usually the very reason of the edifice itself.[17] However, the churches in Rome and elsewhere were usually erected in honor of the most famous martyrs, and the altars, when at all possible, were located directly above their tombs; or the relics were transferred to churches prepared for their reception. In these churches was erected a table altar or an altar oblong in size resembling a tomb. These altars took the form of a table, usually rectangular in shape, supported by columns, one to five or more in number, or the form of a chest, from which later developed the solid massive altar in the shape of a tomb. It appears, however, that from the fourth century onwards many forms were in use, varying according to the different localities, periods, and tastes.[18]

The oldest form of chest altar is the *Confessio.* By *Confessio* was meant an altar built over the grave of a saint. As martyrs were confessors of the faith, Christians who had "confessed" Christ before men at the cost of their lives, the name *Confessio* was applied to their last resting place, when, as happened frequently after the fourth century,

15 *Sermo 310, In Natali Cypriani Martyris,* II, cap. 2, n. 2, Migne, *P. L.,* XXXVIII, 1413.

16 *Peristephanon,* Hymn. XI, vv. 169-174, Migne, *P. L.,* LX, 548-549.

17 Schuster, *loc. cit.*

18 *Ibid.,* I, 139.

an altar was erected over it. Up to the seventh century in Rome, as can be learned from a letter of St. Gregory the Great to the Empress Constantia, a strong sentiment prevailed against dividing the bodies or bones of the martyrs.[19] If a church could not obtain the remains of a martyr, it was sufficient to deposit so-called secondary relics, as, for example, some instrument of martyrdom, pieces of linen cloth dipped into the martyr's blood, or pieces of cloth which had been placed on the martyr's tomb. The *Confessio* as a type of altar was used principally in Italy, although a few altars of this kind are found in Spain and other countries.[20]

The ruling form, however, of the altar on account of the universal practice of placing relics in the altar became the tomb-like shape. Table-form altars, supported by one or more columns, continued in use in some instances until as late as the thirteenth century. To the sixteenth century these table forms could be consecrated as altars. The Roman Pontifical, issued by Clement VIII in 1596 [21], prescribed that only those table forms could be consecrated as fixed altars, which had pillars or columns supporting the corners of the table, so that the unction with the Holy Oils could be properly made at the junction of the *mensa* and the *stipes*.[22] Thereafter, consequently, table altars with less than four columns could not be consecrated.

From the time of the Renaissance the altar takes on immense dimensions and is usually decorated with a large reredos.[23] Sometimes the body of a saint, inclosed in a leaden casket or in a reliquary of gold or silver, was placed below the table of the altar, usually visible through a glass covering. This form has been called the sarcophagus altar.[24]

As to the form of the altar, especially regarding its ornamentation and size, the Church in her legislation leaves a great deal of liberty even today. Only general rules have been made, which can be accommodated to any type of altar chosen to harmonize with the church building itself. In regard to the fixed altar the Church takes for

---

19 *Registrum Epistolarum,* lib. IV, n. 30, *Monumenta Germaniæ Historica, Epistolæ,* I, 264 ff.

20 Cf. Braun, *Der christliche Altar,* I, 192-207; Lowrie, *Monuments of the Early Church,* pp. 159 ff.

21 Const. "*Ex Quo,*" 10 Febr. 1596, *Fontes I. C.,* n. 180.

22 Cf. Pontificale Rom., tit. *De ecclesiæ dedicatione seu consecratione,* tit. *De altaris consecratione quæ fit sine ecclesiæ dedicatione.*

23 Bishop, *On the History of the Christian Altar,* pp. 19-22.

24 Corblet, *Histoire du Sacrement de l'Eucharistie,* II, 73.

granted that it will be sufficiently large to hold the host and the chalice in offering Holy Mass. Besides this it is prescribed that the table *(mensa)* must be a single stone-slab, firmly joined to the support, so that the table and support together make one piece. The support itself must be of stone, consisting of a solid mass or of four or more columns in accordance with canon 1198, § 2: *"In altari immobili tabula seu mensa lapidea ad integrum altare protendi debet, et apte cum stipite cohærere; stipes autem sit lapideus vel saltem latera seu columellæ quibus mensa sustentatur sint ex lapide."*

CHAPTER III

THE CONSECRATION OF ALTARS

The consecration of an altar consists in the sacred rite, instituted by the Church, by which through the recitation of certain prayers and the performing of special ceremonies the whole altar or the altar-stone alone is withdrawn from profane use, is made a sacred object, and is dedicated by a legitimate minister to God and to divine worship, especially for the offering upon it of the Holy Sacrifice of the Mass.[1] According to the present laws of the Church, the altar must be consecrated before Mass may be celebrated thereon.[2]

In the Old Testament itself, altars were dedicated to God by special ceremonies. Jacob, before the written law, it is related, "took the stone, which he had laid under his head, and set it up for a title, pouring oil upon the top of it."[3] So also under the written law, Moses consecrated to God and to divine worship the tabernacle, the altar, and the sacred vessels by anointing them with oil and by performing other ceremonies.[4] But if the sacrifices of the Old Law, which were but a shadow of the sacrifice of the New Law, demanded that the altar be dedicated by appropriate ceremonies, how much more does the admirable and divine sacrifice demand such a consecration!

In the consideration, however, of the consecration of the altar, a distinction must be made between the present formula as found in the Roman Pontifical and the forms used in the first centuries of the Church, for the present rite of consecration of an altar in its entirety does not date beyond the eighth century.[5] The consecration of the altar, in all probability, had its origin in apostolic times, although positive proofs of this consecration can be obtained only from the fourth century.[6] The first definite legislation concerning the conse-

---

1 Gasparri, *De SS. Eucharistia,* I, n. 310.

2 Can. 1199, § 1; can. 822, § 1; Missale Rom., tit. *Rubricæ generales missalis,* c. XX, *de præparatione altaris, et ornamentorum eius.*

3 Gen. XXVIII, 18.

4 Exod. XL, 1-28.

5 Duchesne, *Christian Worship,* pp. 403 ff.; Schuster, *The Sacramentary,* I, pp. 144 ff.

6 The decree of Pope Evaristus (d. cir. 100), "altaria placuit non solum

cration of altars is can. 14 of the Council of Agde (Agatha), in 506: "*Altaria placuit non solum unctione chrismatis, sed etiam sacerdotali benedictione sacrari.*"[7] This regulation was afterwards incorporated by Gratian in his collection.[8]

Although no evidence is extant to show that a formal consecration of an altar took place before the fourth century, one is not thereby justified in denying that there was a consecration. No evidence can be produced in favor of consecration or against it. There was no obligation or necessity of consecrating the altar, for Christ had given no command to this effect and the Church had as yet made no law requiring consecration. Nevertheless, judging from many references in the early ecclesiastical writers, we can infer that a dedication of some kind was performed to set the altar aside for use in divine services and to take away its profane character. Thus Eusebius at the consecration of a new basilica at Tyre (in 314) calls the altar, "the most holy altar"[9], but from this description it is not certain whether this character was ascribed to the altar because of its use for the Eucharistic sacrifice or for the act of consecration. A sacred character was ascribed to the altar by St. Cyprian[10], by Origen, who expressly describes it as a place of the Eucharistic sacrifice[11]; so also by St. Optatus of Milevis[12], St. John Chrysostom[13], and the patriarch Peter of Alexandria (d. cir. 381).[14]

That there was in isolated places, particularly in the East, a consecration of churches before the fourth century is evident from the account of Eusebius concerning the solemnities with which restored basilicas were consecrated. The ceremonies are mentioned by him as

---

unctione chrismatis, sed etiam sacerdotiali benedictione consecrari" (Mansi, *Conciliorum Collectio,* I, 631), and the work of Pseudo-Dionysius the Areopagite, *De Ecclesiastica Hierarchia* (Migne, *P. G.,* III, 426 ff.), tracing the consecration of altars to the apostolic times, are regulations no older than the fifth century. Cf. Braun, *Der christliche Altar,* I, 667; Otto Bardenhewer, *Patrology,* English translation by Thomas J. Shahan (Freiburg im Breisgau and St. Louis, 1908), pp. 535-541.

7 Mansi, *Conciliorum Collectio,* VIII, 327; Hefele, *Conciliengeschichte,* II. 653.

8 C. 32, D. I, *de cons.*

9 *Historia Ecclesiastica,* lib. X, cap. 4, Migne, *P. G.,* XX, 865.

10 *Epistola 59,* cap. 18, *Corpus Scriptorum Eccles. Latin.,* III (part 2), 688.

11 *In Librum Iesu Nave, Homilia II,* n. 1, Migne, *P. G.,* XII, 833.

12 "Quid est enim altare, nisi sedes et corporis et sanguinis Christi?"—*De Schismate Donatistarum,* lib. VI, cap. 1, Migne, *P. L.,* XI, 1065.

13 *Homilia LXXIII in Ioannem,* n. 3, Migne, *P. G.,* LIX, 399; *Homilia XX in Epistola II ad Cor.,* n. 3, Migne, *P. G.,* LXI, 540.

14 *Epistola Encyclica,* n. 2. Migne, *P. G.,* XXXIII, 1278.

an old custom, just as the churches were not new buildings, but simply the restoration of the old buildings.[15] The difference between the former and later practice consisted in this that what was done quietly before in the circles of the faithful under the stress of persecution was now done publicly and with great solemnity. If there was a consecration of churches in the pre-Constantinian period, there was surely the consecration of altars, because the consecration of an altar is so intimately connected with the consecration of churches that both in the East and in the West the consecration of an altar was joined with the consecration of the church. Even today this same regulation is effective both in the Eastern and Western Liturgies. The *Ordo* of the consecration of churches in the liturgies includes the *Ordo* of the consecration of altars.[16]

The first definite evidence for the consecration of an altar in the East dates from the latter part of the fourth century. St. Ephræm, the Syrian (d. 373), in his hymn on the "Holy Oil" refers to the anointing of the altar that the sacrifice of reconciliation might be offered thereon.[17] He makes reference to it as an established custom, for it is certain he did not introduce the practice. So also a little later in the same century St. Gregory of Nyssa (d. cir. 395) refers in definite terms to the blessing of the altar, but he does not relate in what the blessing consisted.[18] In the fifth century the writer of the work attributed to Dionysius the Areopagite speaks definitely of the consecration of an altar, who refers to it as a law, carried out by pouring chrism on the altar,—a rite reserved to the bishop.[19]

In the West the consecration of an altar can be proved only from the end of the fourth century. The first trustworthy testimony is the sermon of St. Ambrose at the consecration of the basilica built (in 393) by the widow Juliana at Florence. St. Ambrose does not men-

15 Eusebius, *Historia Ecclesiastica,* lib. X, cap. 3, Migne, *P. G.,* XX, 848.

16 Braun, *Der christliche Altar,* I, 669.

17 *De Oleo,* I, 3, *Hymni et Sermones S. Ephræm Syri* (ed. by Thomas Joseph Lamy, Mechlin, 1886), II, 787.

18 "This holy altar at which we stand, is in its nature an ordinary stone, different in nothing from the other stone slabs wherewith our walls are built and with which our floors are covered. But since it is dedicated to the service of God and has been blessed, it is a holy table, a spotless altar, not to be touched by all, but only by priests and by them, moreover, with holy dread."—*In Baptismum Christi, Oratio in diem Luminum,* Migne, *P. G.,* XLVI, 581.

19 *De Ecclesiastica Hierarchia,* cap. 4, § 12; cap. 5, §§ 5-6; Migne, *P. G.,* III, 484, 505.

tion in what the ceremonies of consecration consisted, but, from what he says in this treatise, it can be inferred that the consecration of the altar consisted principally in the solemn transfer of the relics of SS. Agricola and Vitalis, although it must also have consisted in other prayers.[20] When he built his basilica in Milan, the dedication ceremonies did not consist in the depositing of the relics of SS. Gervase and Protase, for these relics were deposited later, after he had found them.[21]

In the dialogues of Sulpicius Severus, it is stated that it was the custom in Gaul at the end of the fourth century to bless the altar at the beginning of each solemn Mass, but it is not related in what this blessing consisted.[22]

In the fifth century two reliable testimonies for the consecration of altars are extant. The first of these is the inscription on the altar of the basilica of St. Alexander on the Via Nomentana, about seven miles from Rome, as follows: "*[SS. Martyribus Eventio, Theodulo] et Alexandro Delicatus voto posuit dedicante Episcopo Urso.*"[23] The second is the testimony of the deacon John, who in a letter to the patrician Senarius refers to the custom in Rome of consecrating seven altars in the seven districts in which Rome was built. This custom was so old the writer cannot give its origin.[24]

In the sixth century much testimony is available to show the necessity of the consecration of the altar before celebrating Mass upon it.

---

20 "Hæc sanctæ Viduæ negare non potuimus postulanti. Munera itaque salutis accipite, quæ nunc sub altaribus reconduntur. Ea igitur vidua sancta est Iuliana, quæ hoc Domino templum paravit atque obtulit, quod hodie dedicamus."—*Exhortatio Virginitatis*, cap. 2, n. 10, Migne, *P. L.*, XVI, 339; cf. *Ibid.*, cap. 14, n. 94, Migne, *P. L.*, XVI, 364.

21 "Nam cum ego basilicam dedicassem, multi tamquam uno ore interpellare cœperunt dicentes: Sicut Romanam basilicam dedices. Respondi: Faciam, si martyrum reliquias invenero."—*Epistola XXII*, n. 1, Migne, *P. L.*, XVI, 1019; cf. *Ibid.*, n. 2, Migne, *P. L.*, XVI, 1019; St. Augustine, *Confessiones*, lib. IX, cap. 7, *Corpus Scriptorum Eccles. Latin.*, XXXIII, 208 f.

22 "Quo quidem die—mira dicturus sum—cum iam altarium, sicut est solemne, benediceret, globium ignis de capite illius vidimus emicare."—*Dialogus II*, n. 2, *Corpus Scriptorum Eccles. Latin.*, I-II, 181

23 Smith-Cheetham, *A Dictionary of Christian Antiquities*, I, 62-63; Braun, *Der christliche Altar*, I, 672.

24 "Quod de septem altaribus inquisisti, quæ in urbe Roma sabbato Paschæ moris est consecrari, hoc dico, quia maiores nostri, sive in septiformis gratiæ Spiritu decreverint faciendum, sive quia septem regionibus ecclesiastica apud nos militia continetur a qua hæc ipsa parantur altaria, ut singulis benedictio præstaretur."—*Ioannis Diaconi epistola ad Senarium Virum Illustrem*, n. 11, Migne, *P. L.*, LIX, 405.

The Council of Agde (Agatha), in 506, can. 14, specifies that the altar is to be consecrated not only by the unction with chrism but also by the sacerdotal blessing.[25] The Council of Epaon, in 517, can. 26, insists that only stone altars can be consecrated with chrism.[26] From now on the testimony for the consecration is so plentiful and numerous that it is not necessary to give further proof.

The decrees of the councils mentioned above were taken into the canonical collection of Gratian.[27] The Roman Missal, published by Pope Pius V in 1570 in accordance with the reform regulations of the Council of Trent, incorporated this same law making the consecration of the altar one of the requirements before the celebration of Holy Mass upon it.[28] So also we find the same regulation expressed in the Code of Canon Law, can. 1199, § 1: *"Ut Missæ sacrificium super illud celebrari possit, altare debet esse, secundum liturgicas leges, consecratum; idest vel totum, si agatur de immobili, vel ara tantum portatilis, si de mobili."*[29] Hence it is not lawful to say Mass on an altar that is not consecrated. The Holy See often dispenses from some of the requirements of the Pontifical in the consecration of altars, but never grants an indult to say Mass on any but a consecrated altar or altar-stone.[30]

25 Mansi, *Conciliorum Collectio,* VIII, 327.
26 *Ibid.,* VIII, 562.
27 C. 31, 32, D. I, *de cons.*
28 Missale Rom., tit. *Rubricæ generales missalis,* c. XX, *de præparatione altaris, et ornamentorum eius.*
29 Cf. Can. 822, § 1.
30 Gasparri, *De SS. Eucharistia,* I, n. 311.

CHAPTER IV

RELICS OF SAINTS IN THE ALTAR

The offering of the Holy Sacrifice of the Mass and the veneration of relics are altogether different acts so that in themselves there is neither a direct nor an indirect connection between them. This difference, however, does not prevent a relation from being formed between them in the development of the altar, since the altar and the relics of martyrs were brought together through the idea of sacrifice which is deeply rooted in their natures. Because of this it came to pass in the gradual development of the altar upon which the sacrifice of the New Law is offered, that the altar became also a place specially associated with the veneration of the relics of martyrs at first and afterwards of other saints as well.[1]

The practice of having relics of martyrs in connection with the altar is very ancient and dates back to the first centuries of the Christian era. The basis, upon which this custom grew, is to be found in the very early veneration of the martyrs by the different Christian communities. It became the custom almost as soon as there were martyrs in the Church to have the celebration in common of the anniversary of their martyrdom, as is shown by the example of St. Polycarp[2], when the Eucharistic sacrifice was celebrated with the people assisting at it on or near the grave of the martyr. This veneration is likewise shown in the care, maintenance, and protection of the tombs of the martyrs and of the holy relics resting therein. Evidence of this is also seen in the memorial chapels *(memoriæ)* erected in many places over the tombs of martyrs or in the churches built in the cemeteries in which funeral offices were celebrated for the dead.

However, the custom of having a sepulchre for the relics in connection with the altar can be traced back with certainty only to the fourth century, to the time when liberty was given to the Church by Constantine in the famous edict of Milan. The basilicas which Con-

1 Braun, *Der christliche Altar,* I, 525.

2 *Martyrium S. Polycarpe,* cap. 18, n. 1, Fr. X. Funk, *Patres Apostolici* (2 vols., Tübingen, 1893-1901), I, 337.

stantine erected in Rome in honor of St. Peter and St. Paul over their tombs prove this satisfactorily. The decree of Pope Felix I (269-274), "*Hic constituit supra memorias martyrum missas celebrare*"[3], has often been mentioned as proof of the practice of erecting altars over the tombs of the martyrs; but the meaning of this decree is too uncertain and too much disputed to be used as positive proof. It seems to concern only Masses said on anniversaries or other days of commemoration in the churches in cemeteries, or where such churches did not exist, on an altar erected specially for this purpose near the tomb itself. As with other liturgical prescriptions mentioned in the *Liber Pontificalis,* so also this decree probably only narrates the practice that existed in the Roman Church at the time of the promulgation of this part of the *Liber Pontificalis,* which goes back to the beginning of the sixth century. In no case can it be deduced from this decree that Felix I ordered a permanent altar to be erected over the tombs of the martyrs.[4]

The foundation of the sepulchre for the relics in connection with the altar is found in the period before Constantine, but, as it is in itself, it must be considered a creation of the fourth century. The primary reason the sepulchre for the relics did not exist in the period before Constantine in the manner it existed later on was because it was impossible to have it, since there were no permanent churches. Nevertheless it must not be concluded from this that the Holy Sacrifice was not offered during this period at times on the occasion of the anniversaries of certain famous martyrs near or even over their tombs. On the contrary there is great probability in favor of this opinion. The noticeable fact that immediately after peace had been granted to the Church the custom arose to erect permanent altars over the tombs of martyrs, a practice which became widely spread in a short time, makes this view not only possible, but almost certain. The innovation brought about by this practice did not perhaps consist so much in this that one began to say Mass over the tombs of martyrs, but only in this that as a further development of a custom already long existing the practice arose of building permanent altars above the tombs of martyrs for the Eucharistic celebration, in this way bringing about

3 *Liber Pontificalis,* I, 185.

4 Braun, *op. cit.,* I, 528; cf. *Liber Pontificalis,* I, p. 158, note 2; De Rossi, *Roma Sotterranea,* III, 489 f.

the permanent connection of the tomb of the martyr with the altar erected above it.

The oldest examples known of the connection between a tomb of a martyr and an altar are represented in Rome by the basilicas erected in honor of St. Peter, the prince of the apostles, and of St. Paul, the apostle of the Gentiles. From this time on, however, in the fourth century the examples become more numerous.

At Carneas in Palestine the writer of *Peregrinatio ad loca sancta,* a work written about 385, relates that a church and an altar were erected over the tomb of Job, whose burial place had been discovered by a special revelation.[5]

At Florence in the year 393, in the basilica erected by the widow Juliana, St. Ambrose placed the relics of SS. Vitalis and Agricola, which he had taken from Bologna, under the altar constructed in that basilica amidst the great rejoicing of the people.[6] About two years later he transferred the bodies of SS. Nazarius and Celsus from a garden outside the city where they had been buried to the basilica of the Apostles in Milan near the Roman Gate, under the altar of which the relics of the Apostles had been buried.[7] In 386 the same Saint had buried the bodies of SS. Gervase and Protase under the altar of the basilica, which later bore his name.[8] In like manner St. Paulinus of Nola [9] and Sulpicius Severus [10] describe the placing of relics under the altar. St. Augustine (d. 430) erected an altar over the relics of St. Stephen, which indicates the practice in Northern Africa.[11] In like manner he tells us of an altar erected above the body of St. Cyprian.[12]

---

5 *Itinera Hierosolymitana: Peregrinatio S. Silviæ,* cap. 16, *Corpus Scriptorum Eccles. Latin.,* XXXIX, 59.

6 *Vita Sancti Ambrosii a Paulino,* n. 29, Migne, *P. L.,* XIV, 37; cf. *S. Ambrosii Exhortatio Virginitatis,* nn. 1, 7, 9, 10, Migne, *P. L.,* XVI, 336, 338, 339.

7 *Vita Sancti Ambrosii a Paulino,* nn. 32-33, Migne, *P. L.,* XIV, 38.

8 "Succedant victimæ triumphales in locum ubi Christus hostia est. Sed ille super altare, quo pro omnibus passus est. Isti sub altari, qui illius redempti sunt passione."—*Epistola XXII,* n. 13, Migne, *P. L.,* XVI, 1023.

9 *Epistola XXXII,* nn. 11, 18, *Corpus Scriptorum Eccles. Latin.,* XXIX, 287, 294.

10 *Ibid.,* nn. 6-8, *Corpus Scriptorum Eccles. Latin.,* XXIX, 281-284.

11 "Nos enim in isto loco non aram fecimus Stephano, sed de reliquiis Stephani aram Deo."—*Sermo 318, De Martyre Stephano,* n. 1, Migne, *P.L.,* XXXVIII, 1437.

12 *Sermo 313, In Natali Cypriani Martyris,* V, cap. 5, Migne, *P.L.,* XXXVIII, 1424.

A noteworthy canon of the fifth Council of Carthage, in 401, which was taken into the canonical collections of Pseudo-Isidore [13] and Gratian [14], orders that altars, which had been indiscriminately erected in the fields and along the roads as memorials of the martyrs in which neither the body nor any relics of the martyrs could be proved to be deposited, should, if it were possible, be overthrown by the bishops who presided over those districts. No memorials, it stated, should be approved unless it contained the body or certain relics of a martyr, or had at least some relation to his dwelling or possessions or place of martyrdom.[15] This canon is an important proof of the extension of the practice of having the tomb of the martyr and the altar connected in the African Church at the beginning of the fifth century; but it does not state what canonists of the late Middle Ages read into it that relics must be placed in all altars. The canon was rather directed against the abuses to erect altars everywhere because of dreams or so-called revelations, as it is clearly stated in the last part of the decree.[16]

Prudentius in his work *Peristephanon* gives testimony that the custom of erecting altars over the graves of martyrs was widely spread in Spain at the beginning of the fifth century.[17] In the same century St. Jerome defends the practice of venerating the relics in this manner against Vigilantius.[18]

These testimonies give sufficient evidence that at the begining of the fifth century the custom of erecting altars over relics of martyrs was followed in all parts of the Christian world. The reasons for honoring the martyrs in this manner were manifold. Convinced of the dignity and sanctity of the martyrs, the early Fathers of the Church believed it fit and proper to give the martyrs the noblest place in the church; but this place was the altar, the very heart, as it were, of the church where the whole liturgical life was and is

13 Paulus Hinschius, *Decretales Pseudo-Isidorianæ et Capitula Angilramni* (Leipsic, 1863), p. 307.

14 C. 26, D. I, *de cons.*

15 Can. 14, Hardouin, *Acta Conciliorum,* I, 988; Dionysius Exiguus, *Codex Canonum Ecclesiaticarum Synodus apud Carthaginem Africanorum,* Migne, *P. L.*, LXVII, 207.

16 Cf. Ferraris, *Bibliotheca,* s. v. *altare,* I, 214; Braun, *Der christliche Altar,* I, 531.

17 Hymn. IV, vv. 189 ff., Hymn. V, vv. 515 ff., Hymn. III, vv. 211 f., Migne, *P. L.*, LX, 376, 407, 356.

18 *Contra Vigilantium,* n. 8, Migne, *P. L.*, XXIII, 346.

concentrated. Another reason is the relation of their martyrdom to the death of Christ on the cross. Christ is the first martyr; all others have followed Him giving their life for Him. No doubt, too, the early Christians were inspired by the passage of St. John in the Apocalypse (VI, 9): "When he had opened the fifth seal, I saw under the altar the souls of them that were slain for the word of God, and for the testimony which they held."[19]

From the sixth century much evidence is extant to testify not only to the erecting of altars above the tombs of martyrs but also to the placing of relics in the altar itself. St. Gregory of Tours relates many examples of this practice in Gaul towards the end of the sixth century.[20] In the letters of St. Gregory the Great many instances are mentioned to indicate the constantly growing practice of having a sepulchre for the relics in connection with the altar.[21] Thus it is evident that at the beginning of the seventh century the custom of placing relics under or in the altar was undoubtedly followed everywhere in the Western Church. The *Liber Diurnus,* a collection of forms, which dates from the end of the eighth century, although it is made up of older parts, some of which go back at least to the sixth century, is illustrative of this same practice; for there are given the forms by which permission was granted to place relics in the church or altar.[22] Of the early Sacramentaries, the Gelasian Sacramentary has a reference in the Mass of Dedication to the relics of the saints in the altar.[23]

At the time of Charlemagne the liturgical books, especially the Pontificals, which were separated from the Sacramentaries, mention

19 Cf. *Epistola XXII S. Ambrosii,* n. 13, Migne, *P. L.*, XVI, 1023; St. Paulinus of Nola, *Epistola XXXII,* nn. 6-7, *Corpus Scriptorum Eccles. Latin.*, XXIX, 281-283; St. Augustine, *Sermo 313, In Natali Cypriani Martyris,* V, cap. 5, *Sermo 318, De Martyre Stephano,* n. 1, Migne, *P. L.*, XXXVIII, 1424, 1437; St. Maximus of Turin, *Sermo 78,* Migne, *P. L.*, LVII, 689 f.

20 Cf. *In Gloria Confessorum,* cap. 20; *Vitæ Patrum,* II, n. 3, VIII, nn. 8, 11; *In Gloria Martyrum,* cap. 30, 48, 49, *Monumenta Germaniæ Historica, Scriptores Rerum Merovingicarum,* I, 759, 670, 698, 700, 506, 521, 522.

21 Cf. *Registrum Epistolarum,* lib. I, n. 52, lib. II, nn. 9, 15, lib. III, n. 19, lib. IV, nn. 8, 30, lib. VI, nn. 22, 43, 48, lib. IX, nn. 49, 58, 180, 183, lib. XI, n. 56, *Monumenta Germaniæ Historica, Epistolæ,* I, 77, 107, 112, 177, 240, 264, 400, 419, 423, II, 76, 81, 174, 176, 331.

22 *Liber Diurnus Romanorum Pontificum,* edited by Theodore E. von Sickel (Vienna, 1889), nn. 10, 11, 12, 13, 16, 17, 21, 22, 26, 28.

23 H. A. Wilson, *The Gelasian Sacramentary* (Oxford, 1894), p. 139; Muratori, *Liturgia Romana Vetus,* I, 614.

the placing of relics in the altar and prescribe the ceremonies for it. Towards the end of the eighth and in the ninth centuries the situation in the Western Church was probably this that no one omitted to place relics in the altar at or after the consecration of the church, if relics were at hand or could be obtained. Wherever it was not done, it was for lack of relics. Although the depositing of relics in the altar was considered very important at this time, nevertheless there was no strict canonical regulation requiring it, much less was it looked on as such an essential part of the consecration of the altar without which the consecration would be invalid. If there were no relics, the altar was consecrated without them. An example of this practice is shown in the following enactment of the Council of Calchuth in England (in 816), can. 2: "*Ubi ecclesia ædificatur, a propriæ diœcesis episcopo sanctificetur: aqua per semetipsum benedicatur, spargatur, et ita per ordinem compleat, sicut in libro ministeriali habetur. Postea Eucharistia quæ ab episcopo per idem ministerium consecratur, cum aliis reliquiis condatur in capsula, ac servetur in eadem basilica. Et si alias reliquias intimare non potest, tamen hoc maxime proficere potest, quia corpus et sanguis est Domini Nostri Christi.*" [24]

The second Council of Nice, in 787, decreed that in all churches, which had been consecrated without relics during the iconoclastic controversies, the relics should be deposited with the customary prayers and that any bishop hereafter consecrating any church without relics should be deposed as one transgressing the traditions of the Church.[25] Although this canon was known in the Western Church, it had no special influence. This regulation was made on account of the special circumstances in the East through the evils resulting from iconoclasm. For that reason Gratian did not embody this canon in his canonical collection, although he included other canons of this same council.[26]

In the Western Church there is neither a general decree similar to can. 7 of the Council of Nice nor a particular decree except the

---

24 Hardouin, *Acta Conciliorum,* IV, 1220; cf. Hefele, *Conciliengeschichte,* IV, 8.

25 Can. 7: "Quæcumque ergo templa consecrata sunt absque sacris reliquiis martyrum, in iis fieri statuimus reliquiarum depositionem cum consuetis precibus. Episcopus autem posthac templum consecrans sine sanctis reliquiis, deponatur, ut qui ecclesiasticas traditiones trangressus sit."—Mansi, *Conciliorum Collectio,* XIII, 751.

26 Braun, *Der christliche Altar,* I, 539.

regulation of the Council of Calchuth. When the canonists of the late Middle Ages state it is necessary to place relics in the altar, they use to prove their contention the can. *Si placuit* of the Council of Carthage (401)[27], the letter of Pope Vigilius to Bishop Profuturus of Braga[28], and can. 68 of the collection of Martin of Braga[29]; but they overestimate the value of these texts, since there is not a question at all in them of a decree which requires the placing of relics in the altar at its consecration.[30]

After the time of Charlemagne, especially in the tenth century, the testimonies for the custom of placing relics in the altar are so numerous it is not necessary to mention them. Up to the thirteenth century particularly liturgists, historians, and the Pontificals give testimony to this practice; and from this time canonists also add their testimony to prove the necessity of relics in the altar.

Finally the publication of the Roman Pontifical in 1596, which Clement VIII prescribed for the use of the whole Western Church, put an end to the use of all particular pontifical rites. This meant as to the altar that from now on all altars, fixed as well as portable, must have a sepulchre for the placing of the relics in their consecration, since according to the Roman Pontifical the depositing of the relics constitutes an integral part of the consecration of both kinds of altars so that what had been done before only from universal custom now became a general binding law.

Even after the publication of the Roman Pontifical the placing of relics in the altar in its consecration, while binding under grave obligation upon all, was not yet considered such an essential part of the consecration that it would be invalid if the placing of the relics had been omitted; since not all the requirements of the Pontifical are necessary for the validity of the consecration of an altar. Thus during the seventeenth and eighteenth centuries theologians and canonists discuss the question whether or not the validity of the consecration of an altar is conditioned on the placing of the relics.[31] This

27 C. 26, D. I, *de cons.*
28 *Epistolae et Decreta Vigilii Papae,* Migne, *P. L.,* LXIX, 18.
29 Can. 68, *Capitula Martini,* Migne, *P. L.,* LXXXIV, 583.
30 Cf. Braun, *Der christliche Altar,* I, 540.
31 Cf. Pasqualigo, *De Sacrificio Novae Legis,* I, Q. 678; Ferraris, *Bibliotheca,* s. v. *altare,* I, 214; S. Alphonsus Liguori, *Theologia Moralis,* lib. VI, n. 369.

is a sure sign that this question was not decided in spite of the publication of the Roman Pontifical. A definite decision, however, on this question has been given in recent years by the S. Congregation of Rites in declaring that altars consecrated or found without relics or from which the relics have been removed, are considered desecrated and must be consecrated again by the placing of relics in them.[32] Finally this law has been incorporated in the Code of Canon Law so that at the present time the altar cannot be validly consecrated without its having a sepulchre for depositing relics of the saints in its consecration.[33]

32 S. R. C., 6 Oct. 1837, 7 Dec. 1844, 23 Maii 1846, 27 Febr. 1847, *Decr. Auth.*, nn. 2777, 2876, 2880, 2911, 2941.

33 Can. 1198, § 4.

CHAPTER V

THE PORTABLE ALTAR

Portable altars, or altars that could be transferred readily from place to place, have been necessary for the proper celebration of the Holy Sacrifice of the Mass from the very beginning of the Church. These altars were necessary whenever there was a question of celebrating Mass outside of a church or oratory dedicated to divine worship. Very little, however, is known of the early history of the portable altar, because only indirect references can be found pertaining to it. It was especially in the first centuries of the Christian era that a portable altar or table was necessary, it being impossible to erect fixed altars; then under the duress of persecution, the Holy Sacrifice was offered in the best obtainable place and circumstances. St. Dionysius of Alexandria in this regard relates: "*Quivis locus .... ager, solitudo, navis, stabulum, carcer instar templi ad sacros conventus peragendus fuit.*"[1]

When peace and freedom were granted the Church, basilicas and other edifices were erected with fixed altars, thereby rendering the need for portable altars less necessary. Nevertheless, they were not rendered useless, for when it became necessary to celebrate the Holy Sacrifice in places where there were no churches or oratories (as, for example, when bishops or priests were on missionary journeys), the portable altar had to be used as a substitute for a fixed altar.[2] Although it was forbidden to offer the Holy Sacrifice without an altar, yet it was never prescribed that holy Mass be celebrated only on a fixed altar.

The earliest reference to a portable altar in which direct mention is made of its use is in a letter writen about 511 by the Bishops Licinius of Tours, Eustachius of Angers, and Melanius of Rennes to the missionary priests Lovocal and Catihern, who had emigrated from England to Brittany. They used for an altar, as is mentioned in the letter, consecrated tables upon which they celebrated Mass

1 Eusebius, *Historia Ecclesiastica,* lib. VII, cap. 22, Migne, *P. G.,* XX, 688.
2 Gattico, *De Usu Altaris Portatilis,* cap. 1, n. 11.

in the house of the Bretons.[3] The next mention of a portable altar is made by Venerable Bede (d. 735) who relates that in the year 692 two English missionaries to the Saxons on the Continent carried with them sacred vessels and a consecrated slab to serve as an altar.[4]

However, there is indirect evidence to indicate that portable altars were used long before the time mentioned above. Thus Holy Mass was often celebrated in private houses, especially for the sick and afflicted that they might receive Holy Communion. In the fifth century St. Augustine narrates that by the indulgence of the bishop permission was given to say Mass in the house of Hesperius, whose family, servants, and cattle were suffering from the malice of evil spirits.[5] Here there could be no question of a fixed altar, hence a portable altar of some kind was used. So also it is related of St. Paulinus (d. 431) in the letter of the priest Uranius that when the Saint realized his end was near and the holy bishops Symmachus and Acindymus were visiting him, he offered the Holy Sacrifice with them at his bedside.[6] St. Silvinus, bishop of Alciacum (d. cir. 720), likewise in his last illness had Mass celebrated daily in his presence.[7] Testimony for the celebration of Mass in a private house is also found in many old Sacramentaries, for in them are given the Masses to be said in the very homes of the sick. Thus, for example, in the *Liber Sacramentorum* of the monastery of Moissac (*Moisacensis*), about 800, there is found the *Missa pro infirmo* to be celebrated in the home of the sick person, as is deduced from the prayers of the Mass.[8] In fact, the practice of celebrating Mass in the homes of the

---

3 Amort, *Elementa Iuris Canonici Veteris et Moderni,* I, 353-354. In his preface to Part II of Volume I, he states that this letter is taken from the manuscript code *Canonia Diessensis* of the eighth century.

4 "Quotidie sacrificium Deo victimæ salutaris offerebant habentes secum vascula sacra et tabulam altaris vice dedicatam."—*Historia Ecclesiastica,* lib. V, cap. 10, Migne, *P. L.,* XCV, 244.

5 *De Civitate Dei,* lib. XXII, cap. 8, *Corpus Scriptorum Eccles. Latin.,* XL (part 2), 602.

6 "Et quasi profecturus ad Dominum, iubet sibi ante lectulum suum sacra mysteria exhiberi: scilicet ut una cum sanctis episcopis oblato sacrificio animam suam Domino commendaret."—*Epistola de obitu S. Paulini* n. 2, Migne, *P. L.,* LIII, 860.

7 "Sed ille non inscius appropinquare diem depositionis suæ quotidie ante eum Missarum solemnia celebrantur, et psalmorum cantus audiebatur, non oblitus corpus et sanguinis Domini sumere cum signo sanctæ crucis apposito."—*Acta SS. Bollandiana,* die 17 Febr., tom. III Febr., p. 31.

8 Martène, *De Antiquis Ecclesiæ Ritibus,* lib. I, 7, art. 4, Ordo IX. The collect of this Mass is as follows: "Omnipotens sempiterne Deus, qui

sick became so common that abuses crept in and the bishops of the ninth century had to forbid it or to allow it only in exceptional cases.[9]

Also in military camps Mass often had to be celebrated on a portable altar. This practice began with Constantine the Great who carried with him on his campaigns a tent in the form of a church, the fittings of which no doubt included a portable altar, as the participation of the Holy Mysteries is especially mentioned.[10] This pious pratice of Constantine was continued by his sons and other Christian emperors, as Sozomen likewise testifies.[11] Many particular councils also made regulations presupposing or explaining this practice. Thus a German Council, held in 742 under the authority of St. Boniface, the place of which is not certain, in can. 2, forbade clerics to accompany the army, *"nisi illis tantum, qui propter divinum mysterium, missarum scilicet solemnia adimplenda, et sanctorum patrocinia portanda, ad hoc electi sunt."* [12] The Council of Liptina in Hainult, held in the next year, 743, confirmed the above decree together with the other regulations passed at the same time.[13] So also it is related in the *Miracula S. Dionysii* that a portable altar was used in the camp of Charlemagne.[14]

Up to the time of Charlemagne, it seems, the use of portable altars was regulated by necessity and custom. Mass as a rule was celebrated only in churches consecrated by the bishop; in other places only in case of necessity. For that reason the normal way to celebrate Mass was on fixed altars as they were found in the churches. The portable altar was used only then when Mass had to be offered in unconsecrated places. Consequently the permission to use the portable altar implied the permission to celebrate Mass in an unconsecrated place, for example, in private houses, whereas the prohibition

---

subvenis in periculis et necessitatibus laborantibus, maiestatem tuam suppliciter exoramus, ut mittere digneris sanctum angelum tuum, qui famulum tuum ill. *in hac domo* consistentem, in angustiis et necessitatibus laborantem, consolationibus tuis attolat, qui et de præsenti consequatur auxilium, et æterna remedia comprehendat. Per." So also in the *Oratio* "Super oblata" and the prayer "Infra actionem."

9 Cf. Gattico, *De Usu Altaris Portatilis,* cap. 6, n. 8.

10 Sozomen, *Historia Ecclesiastica,* lib. I, cap. 8, Migne, *P. G.,* LXVII, 880.

11 *Loc. cit.*

12 Mansi, *Conciliorum Collectio,* XII, 366.

13 Can. 1, Mansi, *Conciliorum Collectio,* XII, 370.

14 "Solemnis ara tum lignea tabula erat, quæ linteo adoperta modum altaris effecerat."—*Acta Sanctorum O. S. B.,* cap. 20, Par. 2, Sæc. III, p. 317.

to use a portable altar meant the same as the prohibition to celebrate elsewhere than in a consecrated place. The permission to use a portable altar at the time of Charlemagne came to mean not so much the celebration of Mass on a portable altar as the celebration of Mass in an unconsecrated place.[15]

The oldest decrees known, regulating the use of a portable altar, do not go beyond the time of Charlemagne. The earliest of these is a Capitulary of Charlemagne, in 769, which has the following regulation: *"Nullus Sacerdos nisi locis Deo dicatis, vel itinere positus in tabernaculis et mensis lapideis ab episcopo consecratis, missas celebrare præsumat."* [16] The sixth Council of Paris in 829 prohibited the celebration of Mass in houses and in gardens, *"excepto quando in itinere pergitur et locus basilicæ procul est et id in altaribus ab episcopo consecratis fieri necessitas compellit, ne populus Dei sine Missarum celebratione et corporis et sanguinis dominici maneat."*[17] In the same century Hincmar, bishop of Rheims (d. 882), forbids any priest to celebrate Mass in churches not yet consecrated, or chapels not suitable to be consecrated, except in cases of necessity and provided an altar-stone consecrated by the bishop was used.[18] Haito, bishop of Basle (802-822), in his statutes allows Mass in private houses only by way of exception as a consolation for the sick;[19] whereas the Council of Metz, in 888, absolutely forbids the saying of Mass in unconsecrated places under all circumstances, probably on account of abuses.[20] This strict regulation, however, was local, for the Council of Mainz, held in the same year, allowed

---

15 Cf. Braun, *Der christliche Altar,* I, 75 f.

16 Can. 14, *Monumenta Germaniæ Historica, Legum Sectio II, Capitularia Regum Francorum,* I, 46.

17 Cap. 47, *Monumenta Germaniæ Historica, Legum Sectio III, Concilia,* II (part 2), 641.

18 "Si necessitas poposcerit, donec ecclesia vel altaria consecrentur, et in capellis etiam quæ consecrationem non merentur, tabulam quisque presbyter, cui necessarium fuerit, de marmore, vel nigra petra aut litio honestissimo . . . habeat, et nobis ad consecrandum offerat, quam secum quum expedierit deferat."—*Capitulare III,* cap. 3, Migne, *P. L.,* CXXV, 794.

19 "Ut in tuguriis, ecclesiis non consecratis, vel in domibus, nisi forte visitandi gratia in infirmitate detentis, missarum mysteria non celebrent. Quod si fecerint, propter inobedientiam degradandos se sciant."—*Hettonis Capitulare,* can. 14, Migne, *P. L.,* CV, 765.

20 Can. 8: "In locis vero non consecratis, id est in solariis, sive in cubiculis, propter infirmos vel longius iter, a quibusdam presbyteris sacrificium offerebatur: quod omnimodis interdictum est."—Mansi, *Conciliorum Collectio,* XVIIIA, 80.

Mass to be said in unconsecrated places, provided no church was in the place and a consecrated portable altar with other necessary utensils was at hand.[21] A decree similar to that of the Council of Mainz was inserted by Gratian in his canonical collection.[22]

Besides the permission granted through the pervailing law, by custom, or by the bishop, a new title for the use of the portable altar arose in the thirteenth century. This was a privilege granted by the Apostolic See. The first known examples of the direct concession of the privilege of a portable altar are found in the pontificate of Honorius III, who granted it to the Dominicans in 1221 [23] and to the Franciscans in 1224.[24] No proofs exist for earlier concessions than these, so that probably the oldest known grants are also the first. In the beginning the number of concessions of the privilege of the portable altar was small, but towards the end of the fourteenth century the number granted became very large.

The privilege was always personal, that is, it benefited only the person to whom it was granted. To a priest it gave the right of celebrating Mass in private oratories, private houses, or other becoming places on a portable altar. To the laity it conceded the right of having Mass celebrated by any priest (unless the papal indult specified a certain priest) on a portable altar in any becoming place. This permission had far more reaching effect than the permission granted by particular councils, custom, or the bishop to say Mass on a portable altar, for the papal privilege also carried the right to erect a chapel in one's own house, and the right to fulfill the obligation of hearing Mass on Sunday and holydays by assisting at the Mass said therein.

The persons, to whom the privilege of the portable altar was granted, were in the beginning exclusively limited to persons of the higher nobility, to bishops and other dignitaries among the clergy. At the beginning of the fifteenth century, however, the number of persons who received the privilege is much larger, and the limitation as to the persons is not so strict, for then the privilege was granted

21 Can. 9: "In itinere vero positis, si ecclesia defuerit, sub divo, seu in tentoriis, si tabula altaris consecrata, ceteraque ministeria sacra ad id officium pertinentia adsunt, Missarum solemnia celebrari permittimus."—Mansi, *Conciliorum Collectio,* XVIIIA, 67.

22 C. 30, D. I, *de cons.*

23 *Bullarium Ordinis FF. Prædicatorum,* I (Rome, 1729), 14.

24 *Bullarium Franciscanum,* I (Rome, 1759), 20.

to members of the lower nobility, city officials, doctors of theology and canon law, parish priests, monks, and many others.[25]

The privilege of a portable altar was granted to the bishops by Boniface VIII.[26] When the Cardinals obtained the privilege of a portable altar is not definitely known. They may be understood as the *Superiores Episcoporum* in the constitution of Boniface VIII making the grant to the bishops. As a matter of fact in the Middle Ages, they enjoyed the same privileges and to the same extent as the bishops.[27]

The Council of Trent did not make any direct regulation as to the use of the portable altar, but it made one decision which indirectly had an important bearing on its use. In the decree *De observandis et evitandis in Celebratione Missæ*[28], it prescribed among other matters that the bishop should not permit the celebration of Mass in private houses, or in places outside churches, or outside oratories dedicated to divine services which had to be inspected and approved beforehand by the Ordinary of the place. The observation of this decree was binding upon both the secular and regular clergy, for at the end of the decree occur the words "*non obstantibus privilegiis, exemptionibus, appellationibus ac consuetudinibus quibuscumque.*" The decree directly mentions only the places in which Mass should not be celebrated, but since Mass could be celebrated in these prohibited places only on a portable altar, it indirectly restricted the use of a portable altar. Hence all privileges hitherto granted to use the portable altar were indirectly revoked. The privileges of Cardinals and bishops, however, were exempted.[29]

This decree, therefore, of the Council of Trent became the general law determining the places in which Mass could be said. The celebration of Mass in unconsecrated or unblessed places was not absolutely taken away, for instances often would arise, particularly on

---

25 Cf. Braun, *Der christliche Altar,* I, 82.

26 C. 12, *de privilegiis,* V, 7, in VI°.

27 Cf. Gattico, *De Usu Altaris Portatilis,* cap. 7, nn. 6 ff.; Braun, *op. cit.,* I, 83.

28 Sess. XXII, c. 9.

29 Gattico, *op. cit.,* cap. 12, nn. 1 ff.; he quotes a number of decisions of the S. Congregation of Cardinals for the Interpretation of the Council of Trent, in which this Congregation declared the privilege of a portable altar granted to bishops and their superiors by Boniface VIII was not revoked by the Council of Trent. Cf. Benedict XIV, ep. encycl. *Magno cum,* 2 Iun. 1751, § 2, *Fontes I. C.,* n. 413.

missionary journeys and in missionary countries, where it would become necessary to say Mass on portable altars in unconsecrated places to enable the faithful to have an opportunity of hearing Mass. Provision for such cases was made by the special faculties granted to missionaries by the Sacred Congregation of the Propaganda. Canonists were almost unanimous in maintaining that for a grave reason and *per modum actus* the bishop could grant this same permission. The decree, consequently, had the effect of correcting the abuses that had crept in and of preventing their recurrence in the future. The Council of Trent did not forbid the use of portable altars or altar-stones in consecrated or blessed churches, public or semi-public oratories.

The law of the Code, or the present practice of the Church in regard to portable altars, will be treated in the next part.

PART II

THE LEGISLATION OE THE CODE ON ALTARS

SECTION 1

THE FIXED ALTAR

CHAPTER I

THE CONSTRUCTION OF A FIXED ALTAR

§ *1. Preliminary Remarks*

A fixed or immovable altar is a permanent structure of stone, consisting of the table and the support consecrated together as one whole. The name fixed or immovable is given to it, not only because it is a permanent and immovable construction but also because the table is so firmly united to the support that the one cannot be separated from the other without causing the desecration of the altar.

The fixed altar only is treated in this section. Consequently, every reference to the altar, unless the contrary is clearly stated, means the fixed altar in the strict liturgical sense.

In explaining the laws of the Church on the construction of the fixed altar, no special attention is devoted to the different styles or designs of altars, or to those parts not essential to its construction. The details and requirements of the legislation pertaining to the altar as such are given in full. Any design of altar or style of architecture, that can meet these requirements, provided it is in keeping with the spirit of faith, religion, and good taste, is permitted to adorn the church. Hence the various styles of architecture can be represented in the altar, while the architect is given a wide range from which to choose a design that may be in keeping with the general plan of the church building itself. It is the duty of those in charge of designing and erecting altars to learn the essential characteristics of the fixed altar and to see to it that these regulations are fulfilled in its actual construction.

In this chapter the proper consideration is given to the construction of the fixed altar in accordance with the Code of Canon Law and the liturgical requirements of the Church. The following elements enter into the erection of a fixed altar and are treated in the order indicated:

1. The table *(mensa);*
2. The support *(stipes);*
3. The joining of the table and the support;
4. The sepulchre or cavity for the relics *(sepulcrum);*
5. The substructure.

§ 2. *The Table (Mensa)*

The table of the altar, called promiscuously *mensa, tabula,* and *altare* in the rubrics of the Roman Pontifical, and superimposed on the support, must be a single entire natural stone and one not easily broken.

1. The first requirement for the table is that it must be of natural stone. This is certain:

a) From can. 1198, § 1. *"Tum mensa altaris immobilis tum petra sacra ex unico constent lapide naturali integro et non friabili."*

b) From the General Rubrics of the Roman Missal, c. XX: *"Altare in quo sacrosanctum Missæ sacrificium celebrandum est, debet esse lapideum."*

These regulations of the Code and the Missal, as shown before in the history of the material of the altar, are the confirmation of the existing practice of the Western Church from the earliest times. As to the character of the stone itself, it must be natural or pure stone that corresponds to the mineralogical definition of stone. Any hard or compact stone is admissible, as, for example, marble, granite, sandstone, and travertine; and it may be of one, many, or mixed colors.[1] The Sacred Congregation of the Holy Office has declared that slate *(ardesia)* is permitted.[2] The S. Congregation of Rites allowed schist to be used [3], but refused to permit pumice-stone or gypsum as suitable material.[4] Any artificial stone is forbidden, even if it equals the

---

1 Pasqualigo, *De Sacrificio Novæ Legis,* I, Q. 668, n. 7; Van der Stappen, *Sacra Liturgia,* III, 18; Augustine, *A Commentary,* VI, 86; Blat, *Commentarium,* III (part 2), 62.

2 14 Maii 1681, *Collectanea S. C. de Prop. Fide,* I, n. 224.

3 29 Apr. 1887, *Decr. Auth.,* n. 3674.

4 13 Iun. 1889, *Decr. Auth.,* n. 4032.

hardness and durability of stone, as, for example, cement plates or blocks.[5]

2. The second requisite for the table of the altar is that it be one single slab of stone; thus that a table composed of two or more pieces of stone cemented or put together in any fashion cannot be consecrated. This is evident, likewise, from can. 1198, § 1, where it is expressly stated that the table of the fixed altar must be *"ex unico lapide naturali."* The basis of this regulation before the publication of the Code of Canon Law was, first, the Roman Pontifical, which in speaking of the stone of the altar always uses it in the singular number; secondly, custom, which, as many authors assert, introduced the oneness of the stone, the better to represent the unity of the person in Christ[6]; and finally many decisions of the S. Congregation of Rites, in which this condition is expressly required.

The decisions of the S. Congregation serve as an interpretation of the present law, and clearly declare that the validity of the consecration of the altar is dependent on the oneness of the stone constituting the table of the altar. The Code itself does not state expressly that the validity of the consecration depends on the unity of the stone forming the table of the altar, but, since the S. Congregation of Rites has repeatedly made this declaration, it may be safely concluded that the stone used for the table of the altar must be a single slab in order that the altar may be validly consecrated. This condition was especially declared in a decision given June 17, 1843. In the case placed before the S. Congregation it was explained that a church had been consecrated together with an altar the table of which was formed of six small stones so united as if they constituted one form; moreover, a wooden cornice surrounded this table and joined it to the support. The question was asked, *"An hoc altare, exposito modo constructum, censendum sit consecrandum?"* The S. Congregation replied: *"Reiterandum esse altaris consecrationem, dummodo mensa ex integro lapide constituatur; alioquin si hoc commode fieri non possit, parvus lapis medius collocatus consecretur ad instar altaris portatilis."*[7] The same condition for the table of the altar is demand-

5 Gasparri, *De SS. Eucharistia,* I, n. 294; Many, *Prælectiones de Locis Sacris,* p. 202; Blat, *Commentarium,* III (part 2), 61; Van der Stappen, *Sacra Liturgia,* III, 18.

6 Schmalzgrueber, *Ius Ecclesiasticum Universum,* lib. III, tit. 40, n. 33; Many, *op. cit.,* p. 202; Gasparri, *op. cit.,* I, n. 294.

7 *Decr. Auth.,* n. 2862.

ed in subsequent decisions given April 26, 1890, November 14, 1891, May 19, 1896, and November 10, 1906.[8] The only doubt arising in this regard was caused by a decision given by the S. Congregation of Rites, March 20, 1869, to Bishop Moran, then vicar apostolic to the Cape of Good Hope of the Eastern District. He had consecrated an altar, *"enormiter fractum, sed postea firmiter cæmentatum,"* and when asked to consecrate an altar broken in a similar manner and cemented together, he refused because a doubt had risen as to the validity of the first consecration. When the question was placed before the S. Congregation of Rites, the answer was given: *"Consecrationem primi Altaris validam esse, ideoque nec secundi Altaris invalidam fore si fieri vellet."*[9] This decree, however, was omitted from the *Decreta Authentica,* published in 1898. Nor can one deduce any general rule from this decision, first because it is a particular decision in answer to a letter of Bishop Moran, secondly because it is not in accord with many other decisions of the same Congregation, and thirdly because such an altar would cause uneasiness to priests celebrating upon it, for they would have sufficient reason to doubt as to the validity of its consecration.[10] Finally the decree given May 19, 1896, clearly states that an altar, notably broken and afterwards firmly cemented together, or composed of two or more stones, can neither licitly nor validly be consecrated.[11] On special petition, however, and for a just and reasonable cause, the S. Congregation of Rites will grant a revalidation of the consecration of an altar the table of which is formed of two or more stones, provided the other conditions of a fixed altar are fulfilled.[12] The S. Congregation of Rites also declared in a particular case that the following altar was validly consecrated. The table of the altar was composed of two marble slabs, one placed on top of the other, which were so perfectly united that they formed one table such that if one did not

---

8 *Decr. Auth.,* nn. 3725, 3750, 3907 4191; cf. S. R. C., 28 Sept. 1872, *Decr. Auth.,* n. 3286.

9 Gardellini, *Decreta Authentica,* Appendix IV, n. 5437.

10 *Ephemerides Liturgicæ,* VII (1893), 95, in footnote.

11 Dubium III. An Altare, sive fixum sive portatile, enormiter fractum, sed firmiter cæmentatum aut ex pluribus lapidibus efformatum, valide ac licite consecrari possit? Et S. R. C. . . . respondendum censuit: Ad III. "Negative; scilicet non potest Altare, de quo fit mentio, valide ac licite consecrari."—*Decr. Auth.,* n. 3907. Cf. Gasparri, *De SS. Eucharistia,* I, n. 294; Many, *Prælectiones de Locis Sacris,* pp. 202-203.

12 Cf. S. R. C., 23 Apr. 1893, 12 Febr. 1897, 14 Maii 1897, 13 Nov. 1908, *Decr. Auth.,* nn. 3797, 3947, 3954, 4227.

know the fact he would not recognize the plurality of stones. In this case the receptacle for the sacred relics rested on the lower slab because it was somewhat thicker, although the larger part of the reliquary penetrated the consecrated stone.[13] In this altar, however, it must be remembered, the top slab formed one whole stone extending the whole length of the altar.

3. The third condition for the table of the altar is that the stone be entire and not easily crumbled or broken.[14] The table must be one whole stone, without any cracks, or crevices, or any part broken or chiseled off. The consecration would not be invalid unless the part broken off were of notable size, as will be considered under the desecration of the altar. The stone must be of such hardness that it is not easily broken or crumbled. The S. Congregation declared that an altar, the table of which was so brittle that in the act of consecration one fourth of it was broken off, was invalidly consecrated, although all the ceremonies of the Roman Pontifical had been carried out and the unctions had been made on the four corners of the stronger part at the conjunction with the support.[15] If it should happen that the stone table is perforated in chiseling the cavity or sepulchre for the relics, it would be sufficient to place a piece of marble or other solid stone slab on the part below so that the receptacle with the relics may be placed on it.[16]

No dimensions as to the size of the table of the altar are prescribed either by the Code of Canon Law, or by the rubrics of the Roman Missal, or by the S. Congregation of Rites. In the fixed altar the stone table (*mensa*) must cover the whole length and width of the support. Consequently the size of the table of the altar is determined by the dimensions of the support, for the two must be joined properly in order that the altar may be consecrated. The altar, however, ought to be large enough to allow a priest to celebrate the Holy Sacrifice of the Mass upon it in such a manner that he can becomingly and conveniently observe all the prescribed ceremonies.[17] More-

---

13 S. R. C., 6 Sept. 1907, *Decr. Auth.*, n. 4204. In giving this decision, the S. Congregation made special reference to the case *Camberien.*, 8 Febr. 1896, *Decr. Auth.*, n. 3884 in which a response was given in regard to the sepulchre for the relics.

14 Can. 1198, § 1. "Ex lapide . . . . integro et non friabili."

15 S. R. C., 8 Iun., 1894, ad 2, *Decr. Auth.*, n. 3829.

16 S. R. C., 8 Febr. 1896, *Decr. Auth.*, n. 3884.

17 Schulte, *Consecranda*, p. 6; Augustine, *A Commentary*, VI, 87

over, the surface of the altar-table should be perfectly smooth and polished. For the purpose of consecration five simple crosses should be engraved upon the table; one at each of the four corners, about six inches from both edges, but directly above the support, and one in the center.[18] The cross in the center should not be chiseled on the stone used to cover the sepulchre for the relics of the saints.[19]

§ 3. *The Support (Stipes)*

The support or base (*stipes*) is that part of the fixed altar which props or holds the table of the altar. As it was remarked before under the history of the form of the altar, it is particularly by the base or support that the various forms of the altar arise. Neither the Code nor the liturgical laws of the Church nor custom prescribes one definite form for the fixed or immovable altar. It seems that there never was a law determining the shape or form of altars, for in Rome and other ancient cities in Europe a great variety of altars, differing in size and shape, is found in the churches. The Code of Canon Law, however, demands that certain conditions be fulfilled in regard to the support or base of the altar, the shape and size to be governed accordingly, while the style and design may be of any kind to harmonize with the general architecture of the church. These conditions are treated under the material of the support, and the different forms the altar may take.

1. *Material.* The support must be constructed of natural stone with the same qualities which are required for the stone of the table of the altar. It is not required, however, that it be one solid piece of stone. Consequently, the support may be a solid mass of granite, marble, or some other kind of stone, or it may consist of at least four columns likewise of stone, or the side walls only may be built of stone.[20] At least that part of the support at the four corners must be of stone where the table of the altar comes in contact with the support in order that the prescribed unctions can

18 Schulte, *op. cit.,* p. 3; Martinucci-Menghini, *Manuale S. Cæremoniarum,* lib. VII, tit. 2, cap. 4, art. 1, § 1. The chiseling of these crosses on the table of the altar is not required for the validity of the consecration, but is done primarily to point out to the consecrator where to make the unctions in the ceremony of consecration.

19 Martinucci-Menghini, *loc. cit.*

20 "Stipes autem sit lapideus vel saltem latera seu columellæ quibus mensa sustentatur sint ex lapide."—Can. 1198, § 2.

be made properly in the consecration of the altar; the remaining space may be free from other masonry, or the space between the columns may be closed with bricks or other solid material. Columns of copper, brass, or other metals are not allowed. Metallic bases, however, can be permitted, provided the shaft, and more especially the capitals, be of stone, or a layer of stone must be placed in such cases between the columns and the table of the altar, so that the unctions prescribed by the Roman Pontifical are made immediately and directly upon the table of stone and the stone base supporting it.[21] Nevertheless, it is the mind of the Church that the support of the altar should be entirely of stone or at least have four pillars of stone at the corners where the unctions must be made in its consecration, because no mention is made in any legislation of metal, whether precious or base, nor is there any custom in the Church sanctioning its use, whereas in the Code and the decisions of the S. Congregation of Rites there is express demand that the support *(stipes)* must be constructed of stone. If any one should desire to erect a metal altar, he would have to insert a consecrated altar-stone in it, which would then partake of the nature of a portable altar, or would be a quasi-fixed altar *(ad modum fixi)*.

The four columns placed at the four angles to support the table of the altar may be of one solid piece of stone or may be composed of base, shaft, and capital, as is often the case in columns, provided these parts are firmly cemented together in order to form a solid and permanent support for the table of the altar.[22] The S. Congregation of Rites has also declared that an altar, the nucleus of which is stone but is covered with bricks overlaid with a marble crust

---

21 S. R. C., 24 Maii 1901, *Decr. Auth.*, n. 4073; cf. Augustine, *A Commentary*, VI, 88; Coronata, *De Locis et Temporibus Sacris*, p. 104.

22 In this regard A. Fourneret, in the *Ephemerides Liturgicæ*, XVII (1903), 558, makes the following remarks: "Quod autem ad columellas et capitellos pertinet, quid iuris? Nihil declaratur in Decretis; nihil in Auctoribus reperitur, unde singulas et singulos ex uno lapide integro *debere*, vel ex pluribus superpositis *posse* constare pateat. Quum et altera parte hoc silentium non satis intelligeretur, si columellæ et capitelli, præter suam materiam lapideam, deberent et alia gaudere qualitate, ut esset unicitas lapidis in singulis, quin unquam ei allusio facta fuerit, recte concludere arbitramur dicendo, quod necesse non sit columellas et capitellos ex uno constare integro lapide; sed sufficit varias partes eorum ad formam unius cæmento aut calce firmiter coniungi, ita ut quoddam totum efforment, quod ex usu recepto vocetur columella. Quoad formam, nihil præscribitur, dummodo sustentare is valeat tabulam lapideam."

(veneer), may not be consecrated.[23] The reason for this seems to be that such an altar would be exposed in a short time to desecration, because of the danger of part of this stone veneer becoming loose, since it is absolutely necessary that the table of the altar be firmly joined to the support at all times.

2. *Form of the Fixed Altar.* In accordance with the most ancient custom of the Church, the form of the fixed or immovable altar is either square or rectangular.[24] The support may be a solid mass of stone, or it may consist of four or more columns at the four corners with the remainder of the substructure open. The support must be constructed upon the pavement of the church, or it ought to be set in the pavement in such a way that it cannot be moved. Whereas this is not one of the essential elements of the fixed altar, yet it must be observed in order to make the danger of desecration as little as possible.[25]

In order that the ceremonies of the Pontifical may be properly carried out in the consecration of the fixed altar, the support must stand free on all sides, and not close against the wall; for the Pontifical prescribes that the consecrator circle the altar seven times in sprinkling it with the blessed water and in incensing it; and it likewise orders a priest continually to pass around it and incense it during the time of the unctions of the table. This regulation is particularly applicable for the high altar; but for the side altars it is permissible, if it cannot otherwise be arranged, to put the back of the altar against the wall, in which case the aspersion with holy water and the incensation are carried out by performing above the table of the altar what would be done in the back of it.[26]

---

23 S. R. C., 14 Dec. 1888, *Decr. Auth.*, n. 3698. However, if such an altar is consecrated, it seems the consecration would be valid, but of course illicit. For if the consecration is valid when the unctions are made on stone blocks properly put together (*in structura lateritia*), there is nothing to prevent the valid consecration when the unctions are made on a thin crust of marble with which the support is covered. Cf. *Ephemerides Liturgicæ*, XVII (1903), 559; Augustine, *A Commentary*, VI, 87, footnote 6.

24 Wernz, *Ius Decretalium*, III, n. 464; Gasparri, *De SS. Eucharistia*, I, n. 302; Coronata, *De Locis et Temporibus Sacris*, p. 105.

25 Van der Stappen, *Sacra Liturgia*, III, 19.

26 Van der Stappen, *op. cit.*, III, 19-20; Schulte, *Consecranda*, p. 7. The laws of the Church in no place expressly forbid the erecting of an altar against the wall of the church. The rubrics of the Pontifical presuppose the altar to be free on all sides. However, the *Cæremoniale Episcoporum*, lib. I, cap. 12, nn. 11, 13, uses the phrases "quod si (sc.

In the ceremony of the consecration of the fixed altar, it is also prescribed that the consecrator anoints with Holy Chrism the front of the support in the form of a cross. For this purpose a cross is painted or engraved on the middle of the front support, or a cross of metal is attached to it. If the cross be of metal, it is removed during the consecration, or the bishop anoints the altar above the cross. If a column supports the table in front at the center, the unction is made on the front of the column's cap, where the cross is chiseled. If this center column is wanting, the unction is made on the anterior part of the table, where the cross is cut.[27]

The support (*stipes*) may have any of the following forms:[28]

a) The support may be a solid mass of stone work, the exterior of which is simple in style or rich in design. The interior may be left hollow,[29] but in this case the side walls must be firmly built in order to form a solid foundation for the table so that there will be no danger of separation of the table from the support or of any stones falling out from the support. This is the normal or usual form of the fixed altar (Figure 1).

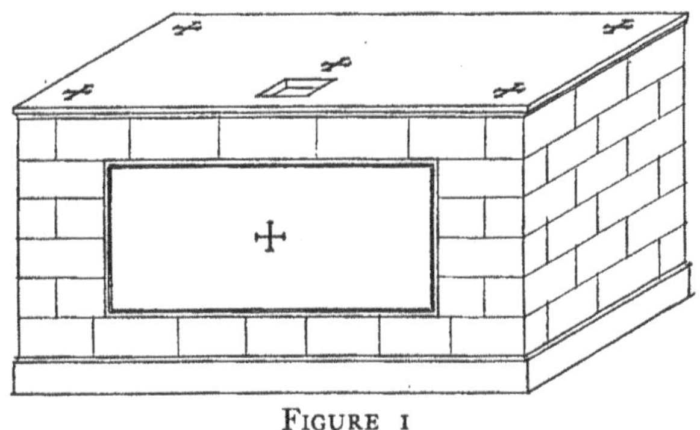

FIGURE 1

altare maius) a pariete disiunctum et separatum sit" and "quod si altare parieti adhæreat" which at least indirectly seem to sanction the practice of erecting the altar against the wall of the church building.

27 Van der Stappen, *op. cit.*, III, 20; Schulte, *op. cit.*, p. 12; Martinucci-Menghini, *Manuale Sacrarum Cæremoniarum*, lib. VII, cap. 3, § 1, n. 2; cap. 4, art. 1, § 1, n. 1. See the illustrations given below.

28 In the designs suggested, the illustrations given by Van der Stappen, *Sacra Liturgia*, III, 18-33, and A. J. Schulte, *Consecranda*, pp. 4-12, have been followed as patterns. Cf. *American Ecclesiastical Review*, V (1891), 430 ff., XXXI (1904), 48 ff.; *Ephemerides Liturgicæ*, XXI (1907), 210-211.

29 S. R. C., 28 Sept. 1872, *Decr. Auth.*, n. 3282.

b) A column of natural stone, as descibed above under the material, may be placed at each corner.[30] The spaces between the columns may be filled with any kind of stone, brick, or cement, or may be left entirely open.[31] In case the space between the columns is left open, such space may not be used as closets for storing articles of any kind, even such as belong to the altar [32] (Figure 2).

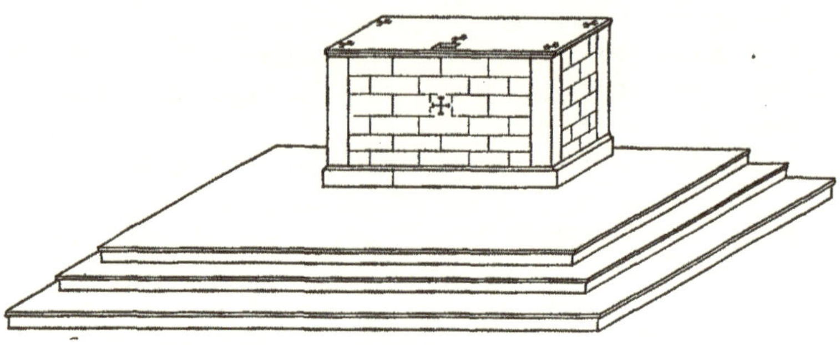

FIGURE 2

c) A column of natural stone, as explained above, is placed at each corner; the spaces on the sides and back are filled with any kind of stone, bricks, or cement, but the space between the two columns in the front is left open in order that a reliquary containing the body of a saint or a portion of the body of a saint may be exposed there beneath the table of the altar at least on the more solemn feasts of the year [33] (Figure 3).

FIGURE 3

30 Can. 1198, § 2. This is a confirmation of a decision given by the S. R. C., 7 Aug. 1875, *Decr. Auth.*, n. 3364.

d) Besides the four columns, one at each corner, a fifth column may be placed at the center in the front. In this case either the space between the columns of the back only is filled with stone, brick, or cement (Figure 4), or both the back and sides may be filled up as shown above in Figure 3. An altar of this kind was declared by the S. Congregation of Rites to be such that it could be consecrated, "*dummodo omni ex parte stipitibus adhæreant.*"[34]

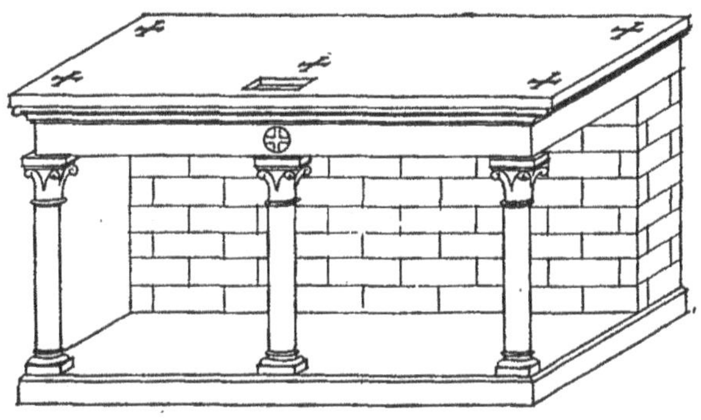

FIGURE 4

e) If the table of the altar is small (it should in every case be larger than the stone of a portable altar), four columns may be placed under it, one at each corner; and, to make up the length required, frames of stone or other material may be added to each side. These added portions are not consecrated, and hence they may be added after the ceremony of consecration has been performed, although such a manner of construction may not be the more prudent because in making the additions the masons or workmen might cause

31 S. R. C., 6 Nov. 1908, *Decr. Auth.*, n. 4225; cf. *Ephemerides Liturgicæ*, XXI (1907), 210.

32 S. R. C., 20 Dec. 1890, *Decr. Auth.*, n. 3741; cf. Schulte, *op. cit.*, p. 6; Van der Stappen, *op. cit.*, III, 21.

33 S. R. C., 20 Dec. 1864, *Decr. Auth.*, n. 3126; in quo S. R. C. declaravit consecrare posse altaria (dummodo omni ex parte stipitibus adhæreant) "omni ex parte lapidea, sed ita ordinata ut Tabula lapidea super stipitem itidem lapideum ex utraque parte ponatur, relicto in medio spatio quodam vacuo, sub quo recondantur Capsæ sacrarum Reliquiarum ita commode dispositæ, ut oculis fidelium diebus saltem solemnioribus appareant."

34 S. R. C., 20 Dec. 1864, *Decr. Auth.*, n. 3126.

damage to the consecrated altar itself or bring about its desecration through the removal of the table from its support[35] (Figure 5).

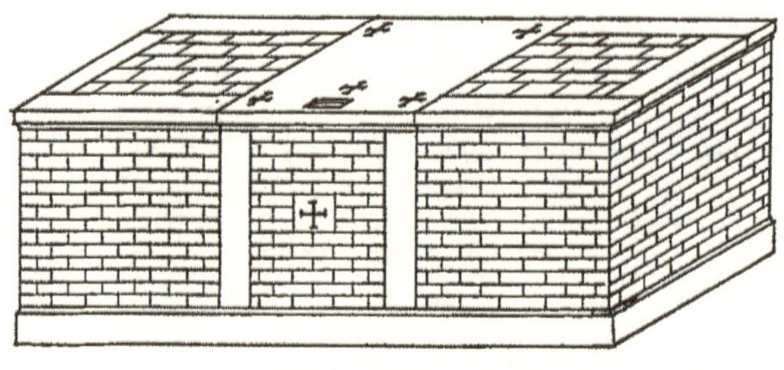

FIGURE 5

f) If the table is deficient in width, four columns are placed under it, one at each corner, and a frame of stone or other suitable material is added to the back. This addition might properly be somewhat higher than the altar itself; and it is not to be consecrated (Figure 6).

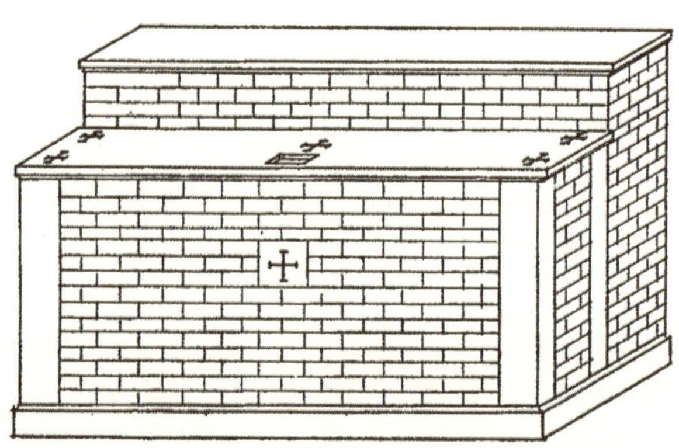

FIGURE 6

The forms of the support (*stipes*) and the table (*mensa*), given above under *e*) and *f*) (Figures 5 and 6), are somewhat unusual, and should be consecrated only in particular and extraordinary cases. It might happen through some oversight or misunderstanding that

35 Cf. Van der Stappen, *Sacra Liturgia,* III, 25-26; Schulte, *Consecranda,* p. 5.

the altars had been prepared in that manner and with everything ready for consecration it might not be possible to put it off. The design given under *e*), or one similar to it, should especially be avoided, or should be consecrated only in case of necessity. This form or concession is admitted by authors, because in no place do the canonical or liturgical laws determine the exact size of the table (*mensa*) of the fixed altar. These authors, however, require that the table in this case should be larger than that used for a portable altar. This case can hardly happen, except from a poor understanding of the idea of a fixed altar, or from ignorance on the part of the architect, or from negligence on the part of those whose duty it is to construct the altar in due time.[36]

The form of the fixed altar under *f*) (Figure 6) is much more frequent, because behind the altar properly so called, a base often must be prepared for superposing some accessory to the altar, as, for example, a reredos or a tabernacle for reserving the Blessed Sacrament. This case presupposes that the table-stone is somewhat narrow in width or is not as wide as the lower structure which is to be used for the altar. The construction should be made as is shown in the illustration; that is, the support of the altar proper should be constructed the exact size of the table-stone (*mensa*), either with a column at each corner, or composed of a solid mass of stone, or left open, in order that the joining of the table and the support may be made by the unction with Holy Chrism at the four corners. This front part of the construction is the altar properly so called; the remaining part in the back of the support (*stipes*) is not to be consecrated and does not pertain to the altar in its strict liturgical sense. This addition for the reredos or tabernacle may be built after the consecration of the altar itself, although such a procedure is not recommended because of the danger of placing something on the table of the altar which might break it, or cause it to become separated from the support, and which thereby would cause the desecration of the altar.[37]

The following dimensions may be conveniently followed in the construction of the high altar in an ordinary church:[38]

36 Cf. Van der Stappen, *op. cit.*, III, 25-26.

37 Cf. Van der Stappen, *loc. cit.*

38 Cf. Schulte, *Consecranda*, p. 7; Wapelhorst, *Compendium Sacræ Liturgiæ*, p. 20.

Length of the table, 10 ft. or more according to the size of the sanctuary. Width of the table, about 22 in. from the tabernacle to the front; from 26 to 30 in. from the candelabra ledge to the front;

Height, 39 or 40 in. above the level of the predella;

The predella in front of the altar, about 48 in. wide;

The steps leading to the altar, at least one foot wide, and not more than 6 or 7 in. high.

The number of steps leading up to the altar ought to be uneven, usually three or five including the upper platform (predella). These steps, including the predella, are to pass round the altar on three sides. They may be constructed of wood or stone. St. Charles Borromeo prescribes that the predella be made of wood,[39] and other authors make the same stipulation,[40] although there is no general law requiring such material for the predella.

The dimensions of the side altars may be smaller than those given above for the high altar, but the height from the level of the predella to the top of the table should be at least 39 or 40 inches.

The question may be asked as to whether it is permitted to erect a fixed altar of a solid stone, i. e., one piece, the usual size of a fixed altar. Certainly such an altar, if erected, could be validly consecrated; moreover, it seems, licitly also, for an altar of this kind is not forbidden by law in any place, and besides would most certainly come under the name of a fixed altar; since such an altar, if the dimensions are large, could be moved only with the greatest difficulty. Altars of this nature, however, are rare, because of the difficulty of obtaining a large single stone and of transporting it. Regarding such an altar the only question that might arise is as to where the unctions would be made at the four corners by which, as the Roman Pontifical states, the table of the altar and the support are joined together. In this case the support is wanting, and, in order that the altar may be morally united with the pavement, the unctions would have to be made at the four corners where the altar-stone is connected with a stone foundation, or they would be omitted, the consecrator having first obtained a special indult from the Holy See.[41]

---

39 *Instructions on Ecclesiastical Building,* chap. 11, § 2.

40 Cf. Gasparri, *De SS. Eucharistia,* I, n. 308.

41 Cf. *Ephemerides Liturgicæ,* XXI (1907), 211-212.

§ 4. *The Joining of the Table and the Support*

An essential element in the fixed altar, besides the requisites already described, is the proper joining of the table *(mensa)* of the altar with the support; that is, the table of the fixed altar must have approximately the same length and width as the support, must cover the whole structure of the support over which it is placed, and must be united to it by cement or other similar material. Moreover, this conjunction of the table and the support must be done in such a manner that the prescription of the Roman Pontifical can be fulfilled, according to which the consecrator anoints with Sacred Chrism the *"coniunctiones mensæ seu tabulæ Altaris, et tituli sive stipitis, in quatuor angulis, quasi illa coniungens."*[42] It is particularly through this ceremony in the consecration that the table and the support constitute one whole, namely, the fixed altar in the strict liturgical sense, because this unction constitutes one of the essential elements for the valid consecration of the whole altar.[43] Neither the law of the Code nor the liturgical laws prescribe in particular the exact manner in which the table should be joined to the support. Hence many authors assert that it is sufficient simply to place the table upon the support, without cement of any kind, provided the table adheres to the support, stone to stone, on all sides;[44] for then it suffices that in the very act of consecration the support and the table are morally joined by the unctions according to the regulation of the Roman Pontifical. In this case the table of the altar must be of unusual size and weight so that it could not be easily moved from the support, for if it should be moved, even momentarily or accidentally, the altar thereby would lose its consecration.[45] Nevertheless, these same authors agree that the table of the altar should be cemented to the support in order that these two essential parts of the altar may be joined permanently to each other and that the danger of causing the desecration of the altar by moving the table from the support may be avoided.

---

42 Pontificale Rom., tit., *De ecclesiæ dedicatione seu consecratione*, tit. *De altaris consecratione quæ fit sine ecclesiæ dedicatione.* Cf. Can. 1198, § 2.

43 Van der Stappen, *Sacra Liturgia*, III, 24.

44 Gasparri, *De SS. Eucharistia*, I, n. 293; Many, *Prælectiones de Locis Sacris*, p. 204; Coronata, *De Locis et Temporibus Sacris*, p. 104; Vermeersch-Creusen, *Epitome*, II, n. 505, who refers to Gasparri and Coronata as cited here; Augustine, *A Commentary*, VI, 88, who cites Many, as indicated here.

45 Cf. Can. 1200, § 1.

Before the publication of the Code, the opinion was held that if the table of the altar, which did not adhere to the support on any side, was consecrated, the consecration was valid; nevertheless, since the consecration of this altar was not performed altogether in accordance with the rubrics, by a special favor granted by the Sacred Congregation of Rites, stone supports were added to the altar and the prescribed unctions were made privately at the four corners so that the proper joining of the table and the support took place.[46] It seems, however, by this declaration of the S. Congregation of Rites that this altar was considered consecrated as an altar-stone or portable altar and that by a dispensation or concession of the Holy See the altar was given a fixed character by the subsequent action prescribed in the case. In accordance with the Code, it seems that the union of the table and the support in the manner described above is absolutely required for the valid consecration of the fixed altar; for since the valid consecration of the altar is lost by a momentary separation,[47] how can the altar be considered validly consecrated if there has never been a conjunction of the table and the support?[48]

§ 5. *The Sepulchre or Cavity for the Relics (Sepulcrum)*

Can. 1198, § 4. *"Tum in altari immobili tum in petra sacra sit, ad normam legum liturgicarum, sepulcrum continens reliquias Sanctorum, lapide clausum."* [49]

1. *Definition.* The sepulchre or cavity for the relics *(sepulcrum)* is a small square or oblong opening made in the table or the solid support of the altar, in which are placed the relics of the saints, as prescribed in the ceremonies of the consecration of a fixed altar in the Roman Pontifical.[50] In the early history of the altar the sepulchre for the relics was often called a *confessio*.[51] A vestige of this

---

46 S. R. C., 8 Iun. 1894, ad 1, *Decr. Auth.*, n. 3829; cf. Coronata, *op. cit.*, p. 104.

47 Can. 1200, § 1.

48 Coronata, *op. cit.*, p. 105.

49 "In an immovable altar as well as in an altar-stone there must be, according to the rubrical prescriptions, a *sepulchre* containing relics of saints and closed with a stone."—Augustine, *A Commentary*, VI, 89.

50 Cf. Pontificale Rom., tit. *De ecclesiæ dedicatione seu consecratione;* tit. *De altaris consecratione quæ fit sine ecclesiæ dedicatione.*

51 See Part I, sect. 2, chap. ii.

use is found even today in the Roman Pontifical.[52] A small stone, the size of the opening, must be prepared to cover the relics.

2. *Size.* The size of the sepulchre for the relics varies to suit the size of the reliquary. The sepulchre for the relics must be hewn in the natural stone of the altar in the manner to be indicated below. Hence, if the altar be not a single block, a small block of natural stone is inserted in the support for this purpose, unless the cavity is hewn in the table. The relic cavity may not be constructed of the bricks which fill up the spaces between the supports.[53]

3. *Location.* The sepulchre or cavity for the relics in the fixed altar may be constructed in any of the following positions, in accordance with the rubrics of the Roman Pontifical:[54]

a) In the upper part of the table at its center, somewhat towards the front edge. This is the most convenient construction, for it enables the consecrator easily to cement the stone covering over the relics, and in the present practice of the Church it is also the usual location (Figure 7);

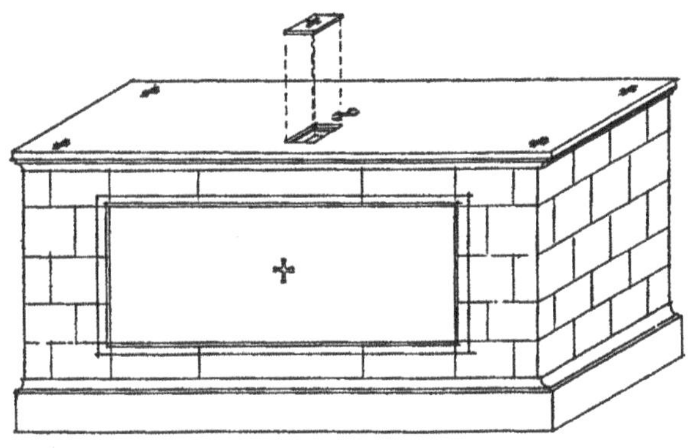

FIGURE 7

52 Cf. Pontificale Rom., *loc. cit.,* where the following rubric is found: "Tum Pontifex, accepta mitra, intingit pollicem dexteræ manus in sanctum Chrisma, et cum eo signat *confessionem,* id est, sepulcrum altaris, in quo Reliquiæ sunt reponendæ."

53 Van der Stappen, *Sacra Liturgia,* III, 33; Schulte, *Consecranda,* p. 10.

54 Pontificale Rom., tit. *De Consecratione Altaris cuius sepulcrum Reliquiarum est in medio summitatis stipitis.*

b) At the front of the altar, if its support be a solid mass, midway between its table and foot (Figure 8);

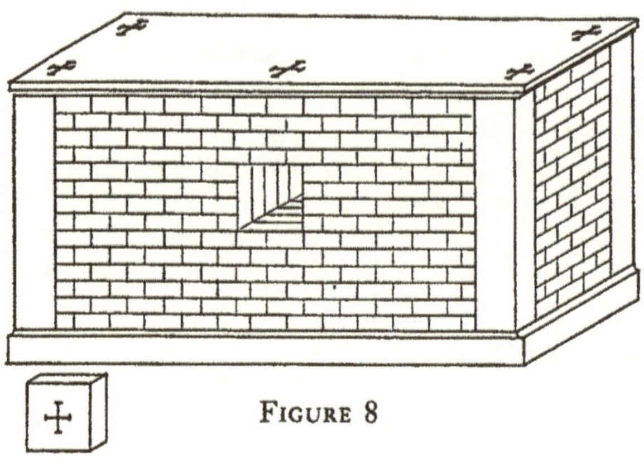

FIGURE 8

c) At the back of the altar, if its support be a solid mass, midway between its table and foot (Figure 9);

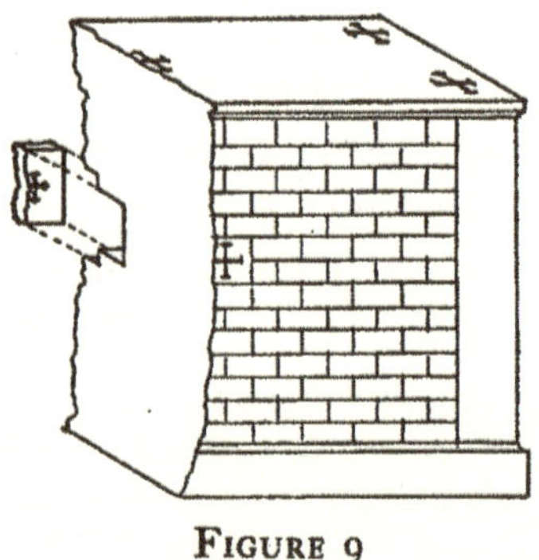

FIGURE 9

d) The sepulchre for the relics may be constructed in the center on the top of the base or support. In this case the table of the altar serves as the lid for the sepulchre, and no small stone cover is needed. This last method is seldom, if ever, used, because of its inconvenience, since it renders the ceremonies of consecration somewhat difficult. Since the table of the fixed altar is usually of great weight, several workmen would be required to lift and set it during the ceremonies of consecration, for the table may not be fixed to the support until the relics have been placed in their proper position. This method of construction of the sepulchre likewise requires a special order of ceremonies in the consecration of this kind of altar, for which the Roman Pontifical makes proper provision.[55] Nevertheless, this much can be said in favor of this kind of sepulchre for the relics that it prevents any danger of desecration of the altar by a removal of the relics or a loosening of the stone enclosing them; although such a construction would render difficult any inspection of the relics by the bishop or his delegate as provided for in can. 1200, § 2, n. 2 (Figure 10).

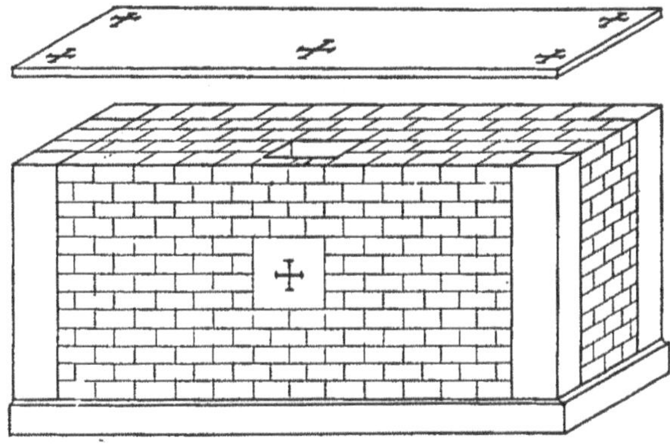

FIGURE 10

4. *Stone Cover.* The cover or lid closing the cavity for the relics must be a single natural stone.[56] It need not necessarily be the same kind of stone as the rest of the altar[57], although good taste and the unity of design would demand that it be the same. If a metal cover is used to seal the relics, although its use is illicit, it seems the consecration is not invalid for that reason.[58] If the cover for the relics is of cement, or if cement alone is used in covering the relics, the consecration of the altar is invalid, as the S. Congregation of Rites declared in a decision given June 28, 1883.[59] This stone seal for the

55 Pontificale Rom., *loc. cit.*
56 Can. 1198, § 4.
57 S. R. C., 15 Dec. 1882, ad 1, *Decr. Auth.*, n. 3567.
58 S. R. C., 23 Iun. 1892, *Decr. Auth.*, n. 3779; cf. Gasparri, *De SS. Eucharistia,* I, n. 299; Coronata, *De Locis et Temporibus Sacris,* p. 106.
59 *Decr. Auth.* n. 3585.

relics must be fastened, not by any material whatsoever (as, for example, wax), but by cement properly so called, prepared and blessed for this purpose according to the formula in the Roman Pontifical.[60] However, in place of lime and sand, which are indicated in the Roman Pontifical, gypsum, cement, or any similar material may be used in making the mixture to seal the cover for the sepulchre. In this case the S. Congregation of Rites declared the words *calcis et sabuli* in the oration are to be changed and the proper terms substituted.[61]

§ 6. *The Substructure*

1. The substructure here is taken to mean the surface, upon which the fixed altar is built, and the nature and character of the construction below the fixed altar. The fixed altar must be built on a solid foundation in order to make the structure permanent. It need not consist of a single stone, for it may be built of any material that will give solidity to it, i.e., of brick, cement, or stone. It is sometimes said that the fixed altar must rest on a stone foundation built up from the ground, but there is no law requiring such a foundation.[62]

Certain doubts, however, have often arisen as to the nature of the substructure of the fixed altar, especially when the church has a basement which serves as an additional place of worship. In order to solve these difficulties about the nature of the foundation below the fixed altar, the professor of liturgy in Overbrook Seminary (Philadelphia, Pa.) placed a number of questions for solution before the Apostolic Notary of the Congregation of Rites. In accordance with the answers given to these questions, the substructure for the fixed altar may be built as follows:

a) A fixed altar must be set upon a solid foundation so that it is practically immovable and fixed, as the liturgical terminology already implies. The decrees of the S. Congregation of Rites require this for reasons of solidity and for the mystical signification given to the altar.

b) Stone, brick, concrete, clay-tiles, or terra-cotta will equally answer the purpose of such a foundation.

---

60 S. R. C., 15 Dec. 1882. *Decr. Auth.*, n. 3567. Cf. Gasparri, *op. cit.*, I, nn. 300 f.; Coronata, *op. cit.*, pp. 106 f.

61 S. R. C., 4 Aug. 1905, ad 1, *Decr. Auth.* n. 4165.

62 Woywod, "The Law of the Code on Altars," *The Homiletic and Pastoral Review*, XXVI (1925), 263.

c) When the floor of the sanctuary is of wood, rubber tiling, or any composition that cannot be classified as stone or earth, it will be necessary to cut away the portion of the floor immediately under the altar if the support is entirely of stone or under the stone columns which prop the table *(mensa)* of the altar if other material than stone is used in the support, and to place a layer of stone, concrete, or brick under the altar or the columns. It would be better in every case to construct with stone, concrete, or brick the entire surface on which the altar stands.

d) If there is a basement below, the pavement, upon which the fixed altar immediately rests, must be of stone or brick; the other part of the foundation may be constructed of solid arches or columns of any material whatsoever, as, for example, stone, cement, brick, or wood. In cases where iron or steel beams are used to support the upper structure, care must be taken that a layer of stone, clay-tile, brick, or concrete be placed between the iron structure and the fixed altar so that the liturgical requirement that a fixed altar rest upon a stone or brick pavement may be properly observed.[63]

2. Furthermore, it is forbidden by the Code of Canon Law to bury a corpse or the body of a deceased person not canonized or beatified below the altar. Those bodies which may lawfully be interred in the church[64] must be buried at least the distance of one meter[65] away from the altar. If this regulation is not observed, Mass may not be celebrated on the altar until the corpse has been removed.[66]

This regulation of the Code is the repetition of the law which has always been observed and enforced by the Church. The origin of this prohibition goes back to the earliest practice of the Church, which is found expressed already in the Council of Nantes, in the seventh century, can. 6, at the end of which is prescribed: *"Infra ecclesiam vero, aut prope altare, ubi corpus Domini et sanguis conficitur, nullatenus habeat licentiam sepeliendi."*[67] The first part of this prohibition as to burial in the church in the course of time passed into disuse;

63 Cf. *American Ecclesiastical Review*, XXXVI (1907), 512-518.

64 Cf. Can. 1205, § 2.

65 One meter is equal to 39.37 inches.

66 "Subtus altare nullum sit reconditum cadaver; cadavera autem quæ prope altare sepulta forte sunt, distent ab eo saltem spatio unius metri; secus Missam in altari celebrare non licet, donec cadaver removeatur."—Can. 1202, § 2.

67 Mansi, *Conciliorum Collectio*, XVIIIA, 168.

but the latter part as to the burial below or near the altar remained intact on account of special reverence to the altar and the Holy Sacrifice.[68] This decree of the Council of Nantes, or one similar to it, was incorporated in the canonical collection of Burchard, bishop of Worms[69], of Ivo of Chartres[70], and of Gratian.[71] The Roman Ritual, as published by Paul V, retained and prescribed this same practice: "*Cadavera autem prope altaria non sepeliantur.*"[72] A number of decisions has been given by the S. Congregation of Rites enforcing this law[73] and even forbidding the burial of bodies below the predella.[74] In like manner did the S. Congregation of Bishops and Regulars and the S. Congregation for the Propagation of the Faith decide when questions of the burial of bodies below or near the altar were proposed to them for solution.[75] The only question which the Roman Ritual did not decide was how near the altar could a corpse be buried without incurring the prohibition to say Mass on such an altar. St. Charles Borromeo declared for the province of Milan, in the fourth provincial council, held in 1576: "*Nec vero in aliis ecclesiæ locis prope altaria (sepultura datur), nisi tam longe sepulcra distent, ut sepulcrale os a scabello seu bradella altaris procul absit, spatio saltem cubitorum trium.*"[76] This rule of three cubits away from the altar and its predella was adopted by the S. Congregation of Rites in a decision given April 27, 1877[77], requiring that the corpse be buried at a distance of three cubits not only from the altar but also from the steps leading to the altar; but this regulation was modified in a decision given January 12, 1897: "*Cadavera ab altari tribus cubitis*

68 Cf. Many, *Prælectiones de Locis Sacris*, pp. 232-240.

69 Lib. III, cap. 159, Migne, *P. L.*, CXL, 705.

70 *Decreti Pars III*, cap. 222, Migne, *P. L.*, CLXI, 252.

71 C. 15, C. XIII, q. 2.

72 Rituale Rom., tit. VI, c. 1, *de exequiis*, n. 9 (in the pre-Code editions); however, in the latest edition of the Roman Ritual (Rome, 1925), made to harmonize with the Code of Canon Law, the regulation of the Code as stated in can. 1202, § 2, has been inserted in full without a change of word. This law is found in the 1925 edition under Tit. VI, c. 1, *de exequiis*, n. 23.

73 S. R. C., 11 Iun. 1629, 9 Iun. 1657, 13 Febr. 1666, *Decr. Auth.*, nn. 508, 1030, 1333.

74 S. R. C., 13 Febr. 1666, 7 Iul. 1766, *Decr. Auth.*, nn. 1333, 2479.

75 S. C. Ep. et Reg., 30 Nov. 1629; S. C. de Prop. Fide, 22 Nov. 1790, ad 3, *Collectanea S. C. de Prop. Fide*, nn. 53, 603.

76 Part I, tit. *De sepulcris; Acta Ecclesiæ Mediolanensis* (Lugduni, 1682), tom. 1, p. 100; quoted by Many, *op cit.*, p. 240.

77 Gardellini, *Decreta Authentica*, Appendix IV, n. 5689.

distare debere; et tres cubitos esse fere unum metrum longitudinis, atque hanc distantiam sepulcrorum ab altari sufficere."[78] Finally this law has been taken up in the Code, not only as contained in the Roman Ritual but also as more exactly defined in the decisions of the S. Congregation of Rites. Nevertheless, in cases where deceased bodies had been buried either below the altar or too near the altar from ignorance of the law or through some mistake, the S. Congregation of Rites always required that such bodies be removed if it could be done conveniently; but in cases where this was impossible owing to a variety of causes, it allowed Mass to be said on such altars, although it required positively that such a practice be discontinued in the future.[79]

No bishop or Ordinary may permit an altar to be constructed that does not keep the required distance from the tombs of the dead; and if perhaps an altar has been constructed in such a manner, or if on the visitation of his territory he finds that the dead have been buried below the altar or too near it, he must forbid Mass to be said on it, until the bodies can be removed, if it can be conveniently done.[80] Only the Apostolic See can permit such a practice, and it is accustomed to be strict in this matter. In a number of instances the S. Congregation of Rites has refused the permission to erect such an altar, for example, in a private chapel in a cemetery, or in a subterranean chapel.[81] Where burial has taken place too near the altar or below it by some fault or other, the Holy See has allowed Mass to be said on the altar only when disinterment could not be conveniently done or where the public authority had forbidden such removal.[82]

When the altar is separated from the tomb or place of burial by a room or stone chamber, it is not forbidden to say Mass on such an altar; for underground crypts of this kind have never been prohibited;[83] moreover, the S. Congregation of Rites has declared in two

---

78 Ad 2, *Decr. Auth.*, n. 3944.

79 S. C. de Prop. Fide, 22 Nov. 1790, ad 3, *Collectanea*, n. 603; S. R. C., 2 Apr. 1875, 30 Aug. 1901, *Decr. Auth.*, nn. 3339, 4082.

80 Gasparri, *De SS. Eucharistia*, I, n. 305.

81 S. R. C., 28 Sept. 1872, 21 Apr. 1873, 19 Iun. 1908, *Decr. Auth.*, nn. 3283, 3294, 4220; Gardellini, *Decreta Authentica*, n. 2208.

82 S. C. de Prop. Fide, 22 Nov. 1790, ad 3, *Collectanea*, n. 603; S. R. C., 2 Apr. 1875, *Decr. Auth.*, n. 3339.

83 *Prælectiones de Locis Sacris*, p. 241.

decisions that this practice is not forbidden.[84]

The distance of one meter away from the altar must be taken in the strict sense; for in one instance where it was asked of the S. Congregation of Rites if a distance of eighty or ninety centimeters away from the altar was sufficient, the S. Congregation declared that the decree, given January 12 1897, prescribing the distance of one meter from the altar, must be observed.[85] The distance of one meter is to be measured in every direction from the altar. The same distance must be observed also in cemeteries, vaults, and subterranean chapels, whether they belong to religious or seculars.[86] Since the Code itself forbids Mass to be celebrated on such an altar, until the corpse has been removed, the opinion can no longer be held that it is not forbidden to celebrate on it until the bishop or Ordinary issues a prohibition to such an effect.[87] In this prohibition to bury a corpse below or too near the altar, no exception is made; hence no corpse whatsoever, whether it be a simple layman, bishop, or Cardinal, may be buried below the altar.[88]

---

84 S. R. C., 27 Iul. 1878, ad 2, 18 Iul. 1902, ad 5, *Decr. Auth.*, nn. 3460, 4100. Cf. Augustine, *A Commentary,* VI, 98; Blat, *Commentarium,* III (part 2), 70 f.; Coronata, *De Locis et Temporibus Sacris,* pp. 96 f.

85 S. R. C., 30 Aug. 1901, ad 2, *Decr. Auth.*, n. 4082.

86 S. R. C., 28 Sept. 1872, 21 Apr. 1873, *Decr. Auth.*, nn. 3283, 3294.

87 Coronata, *op. cit.*, p. 97, footnote 1; cf. Many, *Prælectiones de Locis Sacris,* p. 241.

88 Blat, *Commentarium,* III (part 2), 70.

CHAPTER II

THE CONSECRATION OF A FIXED ALTAR

§ *1. The Necessity of Consecration*

1. The altar must be consecrated before one is permitted to celebrate Mass upon it, so that it is not lawful to say Mass on an unconsecrated altar. This follows:

a) From can. 1199, § 1. *"Ut Missæ sacrificium super illud celebrari possit, altare debet esse, secundum liturgicas leges, consecratum; idest vel totum, si agatur de immobili, vel ara tantum portatilis, si de mobili."*[1]

b) From the General Rubrics of the Roman Missal, c. XX: *"Altare, in quo sacrosanctum Missæ sacrificium celebrandum est, debet esse lapideum, et ab episcopo, sive abbate facultatem a Sede Apostolica habente, consecratum."*

That this has been the practice and the law of the Church from the first centuries has been already demonstrated.[2] Moreover, in this all authors agree that the altar must be consecrated before Mass may be said on it.[3] The Holy See never grants an indult to celebrate Mass without having a consecrated altar, although it occasionally dispenses from some of the requirements of the Roman Pontifical in the consecration of the altar itself. Hence the S. Congregation for the Propagation of the Faith, in a letter dated September 2, 1790, to the superior of the missions of Malabar, gave the following instruction: *"De venia celebrandi Missam in locis non benedictis non est cur quæras; habes enim tanquam Superior istarum Missionum, facultatem celebrandi sub dio et sub terra, in loco tamen decenti, etiamsi altare sit fractum, vel sine Reliquiis Sanctorum. Sin autem per huiusmodi*

---

1 "In order that the Sacrifice of the Mass may be celebrated upon an altar, it must be consecrated according to the liturgical laws; that is to say, if the altar is fixed, the whole must be consecrated, if it is portable, the altar table."—Augustine, *A Commentary,* VI, 92. Cf. Can. 822, § 1.

2 Cf. Part I, sec. 2, chap. iii.

3 Schmalzgrueber, *Ius Ecclesiasticum Universum,* lib. III, tit. 40, nn. 35 f.; Suarez, *De Missæ Sacrificio Tractatus,* Disput. LXXXI, sec. V, n. 6, *(Opera Omnia,* XXI, 808); Gasparri, *De SS. Eucharistia,* I, n. 311; Wernz, *Ius Decretalium,* III, n. 464; Many, *Prælectiones de Locis,* pp. 205 f.

petitionem intelligis de facultate celebrandi sine altari benedicto, id quidem S. Sedi non est in more concedere." [4]

2. Concerning the necessity of the consecration of the altar, the following points must be taken into consideration:

a) To celebrate Mass without having a consecrated altar, whether fixed or portable, even in case of urgent necessity, is a grave sin. This is the common opinion of moralists and canonists.[5]

b) An altar must be considered as consecrated, if it has been customary to say Mass on it from time immemorial, although no testimony is extant to prove the consecration either of the church or of the altar.[6]

c) If the consecration of an altar cannot be proved either through the fact of celebration of Mass on it from time immemorial or in some other reliable manner, such an altar must be consecrated before Mass may be said on it.[7] Since the consecration of an altar is a fact, it cannot be presumed, but it must be proved. Proof may be made by an authentic document [8], by witnesses [9], or by the practice of celebrating Mass on the altar from time immemorial as referred to above. If legal proof of the consecration of the altar is furnished, the consecration is not to be repeated; but if there is a doubt, the consecration must be performed provisionally *(ad cautelam)*.[10] Reconsecration is forbidden for an analogous reason as the prohibition of rebaptism; namely, because the ceremony of consecration imprints a lasting character, which can be lost only through the desecration of the altar. If the doubt cannot be dispelled by the manner indicated, consecration should be performed provisionally. This does not mean a conditional consecration, but as the canon referred to says, *ad cautelam*, according to the proper formula contained in the Roman Pontifical; although in cases of this nature, when the request is made, the Holy See is wont to grant the right to use the short formula of consecration.[11]

---

4 *Collectanea S. C. de Prop. Fide* (Rome, 1893), n. 828.

5 Pasqualigo, *De Sacrificio Novæ Legis*, I, Q. 699, nn. 4-5; Schmalzgrueber, *loc. cit.*, Suarez, *loc. cit.*, Gasparri, *op. cit.*, I, n. 311, Coronata, *De Locis et Temporibus Sacris*, p. 108.

6 S. R. C., 31 Aug. 1867, ad 4, *Decr. Auth.*, n. 3162; cf. Gasparri, *op. cit.*, I, n. 311; Many, *op. cit.* p. 213; Coronata, *op. cit.*, p. 108.

7 S. R. C., 23 Iun. 1892, ad 6, *Decr. Auth.*, n. 3779; cf. can. 1159, § 2.

8 Can. 1158.

9 Can. 1159, § 1.

10 Can. 1159, § 2.

11 S. R. C., 23 Iun. 1892, ad 6, *Decr. Auth.*, n. 3779; cf. Gasparri, *op. cit.*, I, n. 311; Many, *op. cit.*, p. 213; Coronata, *op. cit.*, p. 108; Augustine, *A Commentary*, VI, 8 f.

3. In every consecrated church at least one altar, preferably the high altar, must be fixed in the strict liturgical sense; but in churches that are only blessed, all altars may be movable.[12] All the altars may be consecrated as fixed altars; moreover, it is fitting and proper that they should be thus consecrated, provided they have been correctly constructed. To consecrate a church licitly, it is necessary also to consecrate a fixed altar in the same church, which ought to be the high altar. If the high altar is already consecrated, one of the secondary or side altars should be consecrated.[13] If all the altars of a blessed church have been consecrated as fixed altars, such a church cannot be licitly consecrated unless a special apostolic indult has been obtained.[14] The consecration of a fixed altar can take place also without the consecration of a church.[15]

The church in which an altar is consecrated must be at least solemnly blessed.[16] Moreover, in every blessed church, if there is no consecrated fixed altar, the S. Congregation of Rites has declared that at least one altar should be constructed similar to a fixed altar *(ad modum fixi)* and indeed with a stone foundation in which a consecrated altar-stone is inserted; although all the other altars may be built of wood, to which, of course, must be added the consecrated altar-stone.[17] These conditions are also applicable to public oratories and, it seems, to semi-public oratories likewise; namely, that they can have at least one consecrated altar, or if conditions are not suitable for this purpose, they must have one altar *ad modum fixi.*[18] Domestic or private oratories cannot have by law a consecrated fixed altar; although if an altar is consecrated in such an oratory, the consecration is certainly valid.[19]

---

12 Can. 1197, § 2. "In ecclesia consecrata saltem unum altare, præsertim maius, debet esse immobile; in ecclesia autem benedicta omnia altaria possunt esse mobilia."

13 Can. 1165, § 5. Cf. S. R. C., 31 Aug. 1872, ad 1, *Decr. Auth.,* n. 3269.

14 S. R. C., 8 Iun. 1896, ad 1, *Decr. Auth.,* n. 3907.

15 Can. 1165, § 5. "Altare consecrare potest etiam sine ecclesiæ consecratione." Cf. Pontificale Rom., tit. *De Altaris consecratione quæ fit sine ecclesiæ dedicatione.*

16 Schulte, *Consecranda,* p. 143.

17 S. R. C., 31 Aug. 1867, ad 1, *Decr. Auth.,* n. 3162.

18 Coronata, *De Locis et Temporibus Sacris,* p. 109; cf. can. 1191.

19 Gasparri, *De SS. Eucharistia,* I, n. 284, who cites a decision of the S. Congregation of Rites, given in *Thelesina seu Corretana,* 24 May 1895.

§ 2. *The Consecrating Minister*

Consecrations in general are by law reserved to bishops, so that those who lack the episcopal character cannot validly administer them, unless they are permitted to do so by reason of an apostolic indult or by special concession of the law.[20] The episcopal character, therefore, seems to be necessary for the valid and licit conducting of consecrations. Wherefore authors teach that bishops elect are not capable of functioning in this respect until they have received the episcopal consecration.[21]

The consecrating minister of fixed altars in particular is regulated by canons 1199, § 2 and 1155. In canon 1199, § 2, it is stated that in regard to the consecration of fixed altars, canon 1155 must be observed.[22] In canon 1155 it is prescribed as a general principle that the right to consecrate sacred places, even those pertaining to regulars, is reserved to the local Ordinary of the territory where the consecration is to take place, provided he is endowed with the episcopal character.[23] Consequently, the Code, as also the former law, requires not only the power of orders but also the power of jurisdiction for the consecration of sacred places, although all consecrations performed by bishops are validly done, even if performed without the consent of the Ordinary of the place. Others than bishops to consecrate fixed altars need an apostolic indult or special concession by law.

In accordance, therefore, with the above general principles and with the concessions granted by law, the following may validly and licitly consecrate fixed altars:

1. The Ordinary of the place, in whose territory the fixed altar is situated, provided he is endowed with the episcopal character. Under the Ordinary of the place are included, besides the Roman Pontiff, residential bishops, abbots or prelates *nullius*, the vicars-general

---

20 Can. 1147, § 1.

21 Cf. Paschang, *The Sacramentals*, p. 52.

22 "Aras portatiles, salvis peculiaribus privilegiis, omnes Episcopi consecrare possunt; quod vero spectat ad altaria immobilia, servetur præscriptum can. 1155."—Can. 1199, § 2.

23 "Consecratio alicuius loci, quanquam ad regulares pertinentes, spectat ad Ordinarium territorii in quo ipse reperitur, dummodo Ordinarius charactere episcopali sit insignitus, non tamen ad Vicarium Generalem sine speciali mandato, firmo iure S. R. E. Cardinalium consecrandi ecclesiam et altaria sui tituli."—Can. 1155, § 1.

of the foregoing, the apostolic administrator, vicars and prefects apostolic, and the vicar-capitular or administrator during the vacancy of a see.[24] Those Ordinaries of places, however, who are not bishops (except abbots and prelates *nullius*), are excluded from consecrating fixed altars by virtue of canon 1155. The vicar-general is also excluded. However, a vicar-general, who is endowed with the episcopal character, may consecrate fixed altars by special commission of the Ordinary of the place, which should be repeated every time a consecration is to take place.[25] The vicar-capitular or administrator, if he is a bishop, during the vacancy of a see may also consecrate fixed altars. The Ordinary of the territory, even if he is not a bishop, can give permission to any bishop of the same rite to perform consecrations within his own territory.[26]

2. Cardinals, even if they are not bishops, may by law consecrate the church and the altars of their own title.[27] By virtue of the special privilege granted to them by the Code, all Cardinals, although they may not be endowed with the episcopal character, may consecrate churches and altars everywhere with the consent of the local Ordinary.[28] Those Cardinals, however, who are not bishops, must use the Holy Oils blessed by a bishop. In Rome the Cardinal-Vicar is not entitled to consecrate titular churches and altars of other Cardinals, but it pertains to the Cardinal who enjoys the title of the church.[29] The reason of this is that the Cardinals enjoy a certain degree of jurisdiction in their titular church.[30] Cardinals enjoy this right to consecrate fixed altars from the time of their promotion in the consistory.[31]

3. Abbots or prelates *nullius,* even though they are not bishops, provided they have received the abbatial blessing when it is obligatory

---

24 Can. 198, § 2.

25 Can. 1155, § 1. Cf. Augustine, *A Commentary,* VI, 4.

26 Can. 1155, § 2.

27 Can. 1155, § 1.

28 Can. 239, § 1, n. 30. Augustine, *A Commentary,* VI, 4, and Coronata, *De Locis te Temporibus Sacris,* p. 2, infer that Cardinals need episcopal consecration to consecrate churches and altars. The wording of the Code does not imply this condition at all; the exception made in can. 239, § 1, n. 20, is that Cardinals cannot consecrate the Holy Oils unless they are bishops. Cf. Vermeersch-Creusen, *Epitome,* II, n. 506; Blat, *Commentarium,* III, (part 2), 64; Chelodi, *Ius de Personis,* n. 158, *c*).

29 S. R. C., 30 Ian. 1879, *Decr. Auth.,* n. 3478. Also can. 1155, § 1.

30 Gasparri, *De SS. Eucharistia,* I, n. 312.

31 Can. 239, § 1.

on them to receive it, can consecrate churches and fixed altars within their territory.[32] Other abbots do not enjoy this privilege of consecrating fixed altars; hence they need an apostolic indult to perform such consecrations [33], although many examples of such a grant are found in the history of the Church.[34]

Moreover, since the fixed altar is consecrated in the very act of the consecration of the church, the consecrating minister of the church is also the consecrating minister of the altar. Although the consecration of a church is valid if the altar is not consecrated, such a consecration, however, is illicit unless an apostolic indult for this purpose has been obtained.[35] Consequently, those, who have the right to consecrate churches, have the right to consecrate fixed altars. According to the Code those who have the right to consecrate churches are also as listed above, so that in law there is practically no distinction made between the consecrator of a church and the consecrator of a fixed altar. The consecration of an altar can take place apart from the consecration of a church, as is clearly implied in the law of the Code and in the rubrics of the Roman Pontifical. However, the indult of consecrating altars can be more easily obtained than that of consecrating churches.[36] This is especially illustrated in the formula of the quinquennial faculties usually granted by the Holy See to local Ordinaries. Among the faculties granted by the S. Congregation of Rites is that of delegating a priest—constituted in some ecclesiastical dignity—to consecrate fixed and portable altars, but not to consecrate churches.[37]

It pertains also to the Ordinary of the place to consecrate fixed altars in the churches or oratories of regulars. If the Ordinary of the place is not a bishop, it is his right to give permission to any bishop of the same rite to perform the consecration of altars in the churches or oratories of regulars even if the superior of the regulars should be a bishop. In this case the permission of the major superior of the regulars is also needed.[38] Under the former law if

32 Can. 323, § 2.

33 Cf. Augustine, *A Commentary,* III, 353; VI, 5.

34 Benedict XIV, *De Synodo Diœcesana,* lib. XIII, cap. 15, n. 2; Benedict XIV, ep. *"Ex tuis precibus,"* 16 Nov. 1748, *Fontes I. C.,* n. 393.

35 S. R. C., 8 Iun. 1896, ad 1, *Decr. Auth.,* n. 3907.

36 Gasparri, *op. cit.,* I, n. 156.

37 Vermeersch-Creusen, *Epitome,* II, appendix, n. 871.

38 Can. 1157.

the local Ordinary refused to perform the consecration of a church or an altar for regulars, after they had asked him several times with due reverence and courtesy, they were permitted to call in another bishop.[39] It seems that since the publication of the Code this right can no longer be used, for the Code makes no reference to it and makes no exception in the law.[40] If difficulties should arise between the bishop or the Ordinary of the place and the regulars over the consecration of altars, the regulars would have to take recourse to the Holy See to have the questions under dispute settled. However, from can. 337, § 1, the consent of the Ordinary of the place may be reasonably presumed; but to avoid dissensions and misunderstandings it is better to obtain his express permission as required by law.

One and the same bishop must perform the function of consecration from the beginning to the end, so that it is unlawful to distribute the ceremonies among several bishops.[41] However, in consecrating a church with many altars, or in consecrating several altars at the same time apart from the consecration of a church, by special faculty or indult from the Holy See, the consecrator may be assisted by other bishops. The history of the Church presents many examples of the consecration of a church in which the consecrator was assisted by other bishops when several altars were to be consecrated. The granting of this special faculty or indult is reserved to the Roman Pontiff, and hence bishops or other prelates, who wish to make use of such a faculty, must apply to the Holy See for it.[42]

§ 3. *Relics for the Fixed Altar*

1. *Necessity of placing relics in the Altar.* It is prescribed in the consecration of fixed and portable altars that the relics of saints be placed in the sepulchre prepared to receive them. This is certain:

---

39 Leo X (In Conc. Lateranen. V) const. *Dum Intra,* 19 Dec. 1515, § 12, *Fontes I. C.,* n. 72; cf. Gasparri, *op. cit.,* I, n. 157; Augustine, *A Commentary,* VI, 4.

40 Vermeersch-Creusen, *Epitome,* II, n. 471; Blat, *Commentarium,* III (part 2), 3. Vermeersch-Creusen, *loc. cit.,* maintains that this law was revoked by the Council of Trent (Sess. VI, *de reformatione,* c. 5; Sess. XIV, *de reformatione,* c. 2). Gasparri, *De SS. Eucharistia,* I, n. 157, before the Code, maintained the contrary opinion, in support of which he cites many authors of weight, as, for example, Giraldi, *Expositio Iuris Pontificii,* Pars I, sec. 598.

41 Schulte, *Consecranda,* p. 143.

42 Cf. *Ephemerides Liturgicæ,* V (1891), 246-250.

a) From the universal custom of the Church both in the East and in the West observed from the first centuries of Christianity, to which reference has been made before under the history of placing relics in the altar.[43] An evidence of this is the prayer which the priest says at the beginning of Mass after he ascends the altar: *"Oramus te, Domine, per merita sanctorum tuorum, quorum reliquiæ hic sunt."* This same practice is also indicated in the Decretals of Gregory IX,[44] in which the *sigillum* is taken to signify the small stone which covers the sepulchre for the relics.

b) From the express command of the Roman Pontifical which, in the rubrics designating what is to be prepared for the consecration of a church or of an altar, prescribes that the relics be prepared the day preceding the consecration by inclosing them in a suitable receptacle and that they be placed in the special sepulchre constructed for them on the day of consecration.[45]

c) From the Code of Canon Law, can. 1198, § 4, which confirms the above practice and precept of the Roman Pontifical: *"Tum in altari immobili tum in petra sacra, sit ad normam legum liturgicarum, sepulcrum continens reliquias Sanctorum, lapide clausum."* The Code does not give the particulars about the depositing of the relics in the altar, but refers to the laws of the sacred liturgy, which retain their force,[46] except where a change or correction is expressly made.

Morover, the necessity of placing relics in the altar is of such a nature that consecration of the altar without relics is invalid.[47] This is deduced from the constant practice of the Church that, when relics are removed from the altar, it is considered as desecrated and must be consecrated again before Mass may be celebrated on it.[48] The Sacred Congregation of Rites has given a number of decisions

43 Part I, sec. 2, chap. iv. Cf. Gasparri, *De SS. Eucharistia,* I, n. 323; Many, *Prælectiones de Locis Sacris,* p. 207.

44 C. 1, X, *de consecratione ecclesiæ vel altaris,* III, 40.

45 Pontificale Rom., tit. *De ecclesiæ dedicatione seu consecratione;* tit. *De altaris consecratione quæ fit sine ecclesiæ dedicatione;* tit. *De altaris portatilis consecratione.*

46 Can. 2.

47 Gasparri, *op. cit.,* I, n. 324; Many, *op. cit.,* p. 207; Coronata, *De Locis et Temporibus Sacris,* p. 105; Augustine, *A Commentary,* VI, 90.

48 C. 1, X, *de consecratione ecclesiæ vel altaris,* III, 40. This law is reaffirmed and clearly stated in can. 1200, § 2, n. 2.

to support this opinion, especially in its instruction to the Bishop of Rennes, October 6, 1837.[49] Consequently, the opinion, held formerly by many authors,[50] maintaining that relics are not required for the validity of consecration, is no longer tenable.

Therefore, an apostolic indult is necessary to consecrate an altar validly without relics, or to say Mass licitly upon an altar not having relics. Although this indult is rarely and only with difficulty obtained, nevertheless examples of such an indult are not wanting, for the S. Congregation for the Propagation of the Faith has been accustomed to grant to missionaries under its jurisdiction the faculty of celebrating Mass on altars without relics in extraordinary circumstances or in times of persecution or under other hardships when no other altars were at hand.[51] In the formula of faculties which this Congregation is wont at the present time to grant to Ordinaries under its jurisdiction is the faculty of permitting their missionaries to celebrate Mass on an altar without relics of the saints in case of necessity.[52]

2. *Qualities of the Relics.*

a) The relics to be deposited in the altar must be relics of saints, for the priest says in the Mass: *"Per merita Sanctorum quorum reliquiæ hic sunt."* Relics of the blessed, that is, of those servants of God who have been only beatified and not as yet canonized, may not be used, since the texts of the Pontifical and the Missal refer only to the relics of saints.[53]

b) The relics of several saints must be placed in the altar. One or more relics of the same saint do not suffice. This follows from the texts referred to above, in which the plural number is used. This

---

49 S. R. C., 6 Oct. 1837, Dec. 1851, *Decr. Auth.*, nn. 2777, 2991.

50 De Lugo, *De Sacramento Eucharistiæ,* Disput. XX, sec. III, n. 75; Suarez, *Tractatus de Missæ Sacrificio,* Disput. LXXXI, sec. V, n. 5 (*Opera Omnia,* XXI, 808); Pasqualigo, *De Sacrificio Novæ Legis,* I, Q. 678; moreover, St. Alphonsus Liguori, *Theologia Moralis,* lib. VI, n. 369, says this opinion is the more common one, although he did not subscribe to it.

51 S. C. S. Off., 14 Maii 1681; S. C. de Prop. Fide, 14 Ian. 1802; Decr. S. C. de Prop. Fide, 8 Iul. 1838; *Collectanea S. C. de Prop. Fide,* I, nn. 223, 660, 869.

52 "Permittendi suis missionariis ut Missam celebrare possint, in casu necessitatis .... etiam si altare sit ..... sine Reliquiis Sanctorum."—In Vermeersch-Creusen, *Epitome,* I, appendix II, n. 814.

53 Gasparri, *De SS. Eucharistia,* I, n. 327; Many, *Prælectiones de Locis Sacris,* p. 208; Coronata, *De Locis et Temporibus Sacris,* p. 106.

regulation is also confirmed by the Code, *"sepulcrum continens reliquias Sanctorum."* [54] The relics of two saints fulfill the conditions required by the liturgy.[55] Moreover, it is the general practice, confirmed by official decisions of the Holy See, that they should be relics of martyrs;[56] to these may properly be added the relics of other saints, especially of those in whose honor the church or the altar is consecrated. The S. Congregation of Rites, however, has declared that for the valid consecration of a fixed or portable altar the relics of a martyr and of a confessor or virgin, or even the relics of a martyr alone, are sufficient.[57]

c) The relics must be actual portions of the saints' bodies, not simply of their garments or of other objects which they may have used or touched.[58] Several authors, however, maintain that secondary relics satisfy the conditions of the law, since the regulations of the law and the S. Congregation of Rites mention relics in general without specifying their nature.[59] The relics are placed in a case of lead, silver, or gold, which should be large enough to contain, besides the relics, three grains of incense and a small piece of parchment, on which is written a certificate of the consecration.[60] This metal case

---

54 Can. 1198, § 4.

55 Reg. 40, R. J., in VI°.

56 S. R. C., 6 Oct. 1837, *Decr. Auth.*, n. 2777; cf. Gardellini, *Decreta Authentica*, in his commentary on the decision given by the S. R. C., 23 Maii, 1835, n. 4742; cited also in part by Gasparri, *op. cit.*, I, n. 327.

57 S. R. C., 16 Feb. 1906, ad 3, *Decr. Auth.*, n. 4180. Gasparri, *op. cit.*, I, n. 327, considers the consecration of an altar with the relics of several saints not martyrs as doubtful; for in the first place, he declares, it is certain in past centuries altars were erected not only above the bodies of martyrs but also above the bodies of confessors, and secondly in the case the words of the priest kissing the altar at the beginning of Mass are verified; but on the other hand the words of the Apocalypse and of St. Augustine (cf. S. R. C., 6 Oct. 1837, *Decr. Auth.*, n. 2777) in regard to the martyrs are not applicable. No authentic response has been given by the S. Congregation to cover such circumstances; consequently if such a case should occur, recourse would have to be taken to the Holy See for a decision. Cf. Many, *op. cit.*, pp. 208 f.

58 Gardellini, *Decreta Authentica*, in his commentary to decree n. 4742; to which Gasparri, *op. cit.*, I, n. 327, subscribes; Van der Stappen, *Sacra Liturgia*, III, 29-30; Schulte, *Consecranda*, p. 7; De Herdt, *Sacræ Liturgiæ Praxis*, I, n. 178.

59 Many, *Prælectiones de Locis Sacris*, p. 208; Coronata, *De Locis et Temporibus Sacris*, p. 106; Augustine, *A Commentary*, VI, 91; Woywod, "The Law of the Code on Altars," *The Homiletic and Pastoral Review*, XXVI (1925), 265. This opinion seems to be suported by c. 26, D. I, *de cons.*

60 Van der Stappen, *op. cit.*, III, 30; Schulte, *op. cit.*, p. 10. Cf. Pontificale Rom., tit. *De ecclesiæ dedicatione seu consecratione*, tit. *De consecratione altaris quæ fit sine ecclesiæ dedicatione.*

must be carefully sealed with wax.[61] According to the present practice of the Church, it is not sufficient to bury the body of some saint below the altar, but it is expressly required that the relics be inclosed in the sepulchre provided for them in the manner explained under this heading.[62]

d) Lastly, the relics must be authentic. Doubtful relics may not be used, as the S. Congregation of Rites has often declared.[63] Moreover, it is never allowed to mix doubtful or uncertain relics with authenticated ones.[64] If the relics are authentic, they may be placed in the altar even if it is not known to what saint they pertain.[65]

§ 4. *The Ceremonies of Consecration*

The ceremonies to be observed in the consecration of fixed and portable altars are contained in the Roman Pontifical, Part II. These rites are found under three separate titles, *De ecclesiæ dedicatione seu consecratione, De Altaris Consecratione Quæ fit sine Ecclesiæ Dedicatione,* and *De Altaris portatilis Consecratione.* There is no difference between the consecration of a fixed altar in connection with the consecration of a church and the consecration of a fixed altar which takes place without the consecration of a church. The difference between the consecration of a fixed altar and a portable altar consists essentially in this that in consecrating a portable altar only the surface of the altar-stone is anointed, while in consecrating a fixed altar another special unction is made at the four corners by which the table of the altar is joined and connected morally to the base thus that not the one stone but the whole altar is considered consecrated. Consequently, it is evident that a fixed altar may not be consecrated by the rites of a portable altar, or vice versa; although the consecration of a portable altar with the rites of a fixed altar would certainly be valid.[66]

The rites described in the Roman Pontifical must be strictly observed. No deviation from them is admissible, although all the prayers and ceremonies described are not required for the validity

---

61 Gasparri, *op. cit.,* I, n. 329.
62 Coronata, *op. cit.,* p. 107; cf. Part II, sec. 1, chap. 1, § 5.
63 S. R. C., 5 Dec. 1851, ad 3, Aug. 1901, ad 1, *Decr. Auth.,* nn. 2991, 4082.
64 S. R. C., 5 Dec. 1851, ad 2, *Decr. Auth.,* n. 2991.
65 S. R. C., 7 Sept. 1630, *Decr. Auth.,* n. 542.
66 Gasparri, *De SS. Eucharistia,* I, n. 314.

of the consecration. It will help to note here the difficulties which may arise in the course of the consecration and the decisions relative thereto which the S. Congregation of Rites has given.

1. If in the consecration of an altar all the unctions with Chrism are omitted, the consecration is invalid; but not all the unctions are required for the validity.[67] The consecrator, however, must be especially careful that he perform all the unctions as prescribed, for the S. Congregation of Rites in the decision referred to declared that no unction is to be omitted. This rite of anointing the altar with sacred Chrism is most ancient, and is common both to the Roman and to the Gallican liturgy. Mention of it was made in the Council of Agde (Agatha), in the year 506, can. 14: *"Altaria placuit non solum unctione chrismatis, sed etiam sacerdotali benedictione sacrari."*[68] And in the Council of Epaon, in 517, can. 26, it was ordered that only stone altars should be anointed with Chrism.[69] The Oriental Church likewise has observed this same rite from the remotest period, for the author of the work *De Ecclesiastica Hierarchia* refers to it in these words: *"Hoc etiam sancte observa ut sacratissima illa lex, mysterium altaris, consecrationem sanctissimis perficiat unguentis."*[70] Lastly Innocent III, in the Decretals says: *"Ungitur præterea, secundum ecclesiasticum morem, cum consecratur altare, cum dedicatur templum, cum benedicitur calix, non solum ex mandato legis divinæ, verum etiam exemplo Beati Sylvestri qui cum consecrabat altare, illud chrismate perungebat."*[71] All of which shows the importance of the anointing with Chrism for the validity of the consecration.[72]

2. If the sacred Chrism or the oil of Cathecumens should begin to fail, and the quantity on hand will not suffice, it is permitted to add a quantity of unblessed olive oil to the diminished supply, but always in a smaller quantity than the amount of the blessed oil.[73] In like manner if the blessed water should begin to give out, other water

---

67 S. R. C., 2 Maii 1892, *Decr. Auth.*, n. 3771; 14 Ian. 1910, *Decr. Auth.*, n. 4244. Cf. Gasparri, *op. cit.*, I, n. 319; Coronata, *De Locis et Temporibus Sacris*, p. 110.

68 Mansi, *Conciliorum Collectio*, VIII, 273.

69 *Ibid.*, VIII, 562.

70 Migne, *P. G.*, III, 426.

71 C. un., X, *de sacra unctione*, I, 15.

72 Gasparri, *De SS. Eucharistia*, I, n. 319.

73 Can. 734, § 2.

not blessed may be added, always of course in less quantity than that which is blessed.[74]

3. The Roman Pontifical also prescribes the exposition of the relics of the saints on the eve of the consecration of a church or a fixed altar, the recitation of matins and lauds in honor of the saints whose relics are to be placed in the altar, and the watch to be observed before them: *"Celebrandæque sunt vigiliæ ante Reliquias ipsas, et canendi Nocturni, et Matutinæ Laudes, in honorem Sanctorum, quorum Reliquiæ sunt recondendæ."* The rite of celebrating the vigil or the watch before the relics of the saints which are to be deposited in the fixed altar in its consecration has been taken form the old Gallican liturgy.[75] This watch is to continue through the night and the following morning until the Holy Relics are carried to the church. The Pontifical itself does not demand this expressly, but that it should be done is certain, since it is conformable to the ancient liturgy from which this rite is taken.[76] The vigil consists chiefly in the recitation of matins and lauds of the saints whose relics are to be placed in the altar in its consecration. Matins and lauds are to be taken not from the psalter of the day occurring, but *de communi plurimorum martyrum* with the prayer from the third place *Deus qui nos* omitting the word *annua* and the names of the saints.[77] The lessons of the first nocturn are *Fratres, Debitores;* of the second nocturn, *Quotiescumque, fratres;* and of the third nocturn, *Dominus ac Redemptor.*[78] It is a votive office, celebrated *ritu duplici,* without any commemoration.[79] If the relics are of martyrs who have a proper office in the Breviary, as, for example, SS. Vincent and Anastasius, SS. Fabian and Sebastian, the proper office of these martyrs may be recited.[80] The office *Dedicationis Ecclesiæ* cannot be recited on this occasion, in case the consecration of the fixed altar is performed in connection with the consecration

74 Gasparri, *op. cit.,* I, n. 320; Giraldi, *Expositio Iuris Pontificii,* Pars I, sec. 599; Coronata, *De Locis et Temporibus Sacris,* p. 110.

75 Gasparri, *op. cit.* I, n. 330.

76 Gasparri, *loc. cit.;* Gardellini, *Decreta Authentica,* in his commentary on decree n. 4742; Coronata, *op. cit.,* p. 110.

77 S. R. C., 14 Iun. 1845, *Decr. Auth.,* n. 2886; S. R. C., 18 Aug. 1913, *Acta Apost. Sedis,* V (1913), 399.

78 Schulte, *Consecranda,* p. 28.

79 Martinucci-Menghini, *Manuale Sacrarum Cæremoniarum,* lib. VII, tit. 2, cap. 3, n. 41; Van der Stappen, *Sacra Liturgia,* III, 35; Schulte, *loc. cit.*

80 Martinucci-Menghini, *loc. cit.,* in footnote.

of the church.[81] The recitation of the office *Sanctorum Martyrum* in preparation for the consecration of the altar does not dispense from the recitation of the current office. The axiom, *Officium pro officio valet,* cannot here be applied.[82] It is not required, however, that the whole night be spent in chanting psalms or hymns.[83] Martinucci says that it is the practice at Rome, after reciting matins and lauds as indicated above, for two, four, or six lay persons to continue the watch until the following morning when the Holy Relics are carried to the church.[84] The Pontifical does not mention who are obliged to recite or chant matins and lauds for the vigil; from which it follows that the obligation is real rather than personal. However, this obligation, it seems, binds especially the clerics, either regular or secular, who are attached to the church; although even laymen can fulfill this same duty.[85]

4. If the fixed altar alone is to be consecrated, not the church, the watch or the vigil only must be observed. The ecclesiastical fast *(ieiunium)* which is required on the occasion of the consecration of a church is not prescribed in preparation for the consecration of the fixed altar.[86]

§ 5. *Other Requirements*

1. *Time.* The consecration of a fixed altar, if performed apart from the dedication of the church in which it is stationed, may take place on any day, but it is more appropriate that this ceremony should be performed on a Sunday or holyday of obligation.[87]

2. *Registration.* After the consecration of the fixed altar, a document in testimony thereof should be drawn up, of which one copy is to be kept in the episcopal curia, and another in the archives of the church.[88]

---

81 S. R. C., 7 Dec. 1844, *Decr. Auth.*, n. 2868.

82 S. R. C., 16 Sept. 1881, ad 2, *Decr. Auth.*, n. 3532.

83 S. R. C., 22 Febr. 1888, ad 3, *Decr. Auth.*, n. 3686.

84 Martinucci-Menghini, *op. cit.*, lib. VII, tit. 2, cap. 3, n. 13, footnote; cf. Van der Stappen, *Sacra Liturgia,* III, 36; *Ephemerides Liturgicæ,* IX (1895), 692.

85 Gasparri, *op. cit.*, I, n. 331; Coronata, *op. cit.*, p. 111.

86 Van der Stappen, *op. cit.*, III, 36; Coronata, *op. cit.*, p. 111; Many, *Prælectiones de Locis Sacris,* p. 209.

87 Can. 1199, § 3. Cf. Pontificale Rom., tit. *De altaris consecratione quæ fit sine ecclesiæ dedicatione.*

88 Can. 1158.

CHAPTER III

THE DESECRATION OF A FIXED ALTAR

I. *Definition.* The desecration *(exsecratio)* of an altar is the total loss of its consecration. An altar which has been desecrated is the same as if it had not been consecrated; hence, as it is not lawful to say Mass upon an unconsecrated altar, so also it is unlawful to say Mass upon a desecrated altar. Before Mass may be celebrated upon an altar that has been desecrated, it must be consecrated anew.

II. *Cases of Desecration.* The desecration of an altar according to the present law of the Church is governed by can. 1200, as follows:

§ 1. *Altare immobile amittit consecrationem, si tabula seu mensa a stipite, etiam per temporis momentum, separetur; quo in casu Ordinarius potest permittere ut presbyter altaris consecrationem rursus perficiat ritu formulaque breviore.*

§ 2. *Tum altare immobile tum petra sacra amittunt consecrationem:*

1.° *Si frangantur enormiter sive ratione quantitatis fractionis sive ratione loci unctionis;*

2.° *Si amoveantur reliquiæ aut frangatur vel amoveatur sepulcri operculum, excepto casu quo ipse Episcopus vel eius delegatus operculum amoveat ad illud firmandum vel reparandum vel subrogandum, aut ad visitandas reliquias.*

§ 3. *Levis fractio operculi non inducit exsecrationem et quilibet sacerdos potest rimulam cemento firmare.*

§ 4. *Exsecratio ecclesiæ non secumfert exsecrationem altarium sive immobilium sive mobilium; et viceversa.*

In accordance with these laws and the decisions of the Sacred Congregation of Rites, which form their basis in great part, the fixed altar may become desecrated in the following ways:[1]

1. The fixed altar is desecrated or loses its consecration by the separation of the table from its support, even if this separation is momentary.[2] This has long been the established practice of the

---

1 The desecration of the portable altar is considered separatelv in the next section.

2 Can. 1200, § 1.

Church, for this law is contained in the decree of Alexander III [3] and Innocent III,[4] afterwards incorporated as indicated in the Decretals of Gregory IX. The reason for this, as explained by Reiffenstuel, is that the essential element in the consecration of the fixed altar consists in the conjunction of the table of the altar with the lower structure by the unctions at the four corners in the manner prescribed by the Roman Pontifical; hence, if the table of the altar is removed from the lower structure, or if the stones of the lower structure immediately or directly touching the table are removed, this moral union is broken and the altar is considered desecrated. The altar, however, is not desecrated, the same author adds, if the stones below those directly contiguous with the table of the altar are removed and others substituted at once, provided the altar retains the same height and dimensions, even if successively all such lower stones should be taken away and other substituted.[5] Under this heading it is useful, likewise, to consider the following points:

a) In order that a fixed altar be desecrated, it is not required that the table be altogether separated from the base and placed in another position, for it suffices to cause its desecration that the table be raised from the base, even if this elevation is done to place new cement, or to add stones to the support, or to change the stones adjoining the table.[6]

b) The fixed altar is not desecrated if the whole structure, that is, the table and the support as a unit, is moved from one place to another, provided the table and the support do not become separated in the removal. This opinion is supported by Gasparri,[7] Many,[8] Vermeersch-Creusen,[9] Coronata,[10] and others.[11] Prümmer declares

---

3 C. 1, X, *de consecratione ecclesiæ vel altaris,* III, 40.

4 C. 3, X, *de consecratione ecclesiæ vel altaris,* III, 40; cf. Migne, *P. L.,* CCXIV, 361.

5 *Ius Canonicum Universum,* lib. III, tit. 40, n. 38.

6 Many, *Prælectiones de Locis Sacris,* p. 210; Gasparri, *De SS. Eucharistia,* I, n. 334; Coronata, *De Locis et Temporibus Sacris,* p. 114; cf. S. R. C., 15 Maii 1819, 15 Apr. 1869, 23 Febr. 1884, ad 7, *Decr. Auth.,* nn. 2599, 3198, 3605.

7 *Op. cit.,* I, n. 337.

8 *Op. cit.,* p. 210.

9 *Epitome,* II, n. 507.

10 *Op. cit.,* p. 114.

11 Suarez (*Tractatus de Sacrificio Missæ,* Disput. LXXXI, sec. 5, n. 5, (*Opera Omnia,* XXI, 808), De Lugo (*Disputationes Scholasticæ, De Eucharistia,* Disput. XX, sec. 2, n. 74; IV, 264), Pasqualigo (*De Sacrificio Novæ*

it to be probable and safe to follow in practice.[12] Woywod [13] maintains the opposite opinion and cites the decision given by the S. Congregation of Rites, February 20, 1874 [14], in which it was declared that the high altar of a certain parish church, moved only a few feet from its old location, had to be reconsecrated. This decision, however, is particular and can be interpreted of an altar taken apart and set up anew, for no mention is made at all about the manner of removal or whether the table and support remained intact. The Code of Canon Law is silent on this point, and since it mentions in detail the manner in which the altar is desecrated, it seems to be safe to assume the omission was intentional and safe likewise to follow the opinion that the altar, moved as described above, is not desecrated.[15]

c) If the fixed altar is desecrated by the removal of the table from its support, the entire altar is desecrated so that it is not permitted to celebrate Mass on any part of it or to use the table (*mensa*) as a portable altar.[16] The reason for this is that the consecration of a fixed altar is something indivisible and adheres to the two parts joined together as one. Consequently, when the consecration is lost by the separation of the table from the support, it is lost not only to the entire altar but also to each of its parts.[17]

d) If the table of the fixed altar rests upon four columns and becomes momentarily separated form only one or two of them, the altar is not desecrated for this reason; because as not all the unctions are required for the essence of the consecration, as explained before, and as the altar is validly consecrated if the unctions are made only

Legis, I, Q. 685), Schmalzgrueber (*Ius Ecclesiasticum Universum,* lib. III, tit. 40, n. 45), St. Alphonsus Liguori (*Theologia Moralis,* lib. VI, n. 369), and Giraldi (*Expositio Iuris Pontificii,* Pars I, sec. 599), in their commentaries on the Decretals, held this same opinion. Gardellini in his commentary on decree n. 2600 (n. 4562 in his collection) states that this is the common opinion.

12 *Manuale Iuris Canonici,* p. 442.

13 "The Law of the Code on Altars," *The Homiletic and Pastoral Review,* XXVI (1925), 269.

14 *Decr. Auth.,* n. 3326.

15 Braun, *Der christliche Altar,* I, 45-48. The above represents the theory in the matter. In practice, however, it would seem to be difficult to move a fixed altar from one place to another without causing the separation of the table from the support, unless much care was used and heavy expenses were incurred. Since the Code permits the short formula of consecration to be used when the altar is desecrated by the separation of the table from the support, the question loses much of its importance.

16 S. R. C., 20 Mart. 1896, *Decr. Auth.,* n. 3198.

17 Cf. Many, *op. cit.,* p. 210; Coronata, *op. cit.,* p. 114.

on two columns, so also it can be said that the consecration continues as long as the unctions of at least two columns remain intact. The separation, therefore, which causes the desecration of the altar, must be the entire separation of the table from its support.[18]

e) When the fixed altar is desecrated by the removal of the table from the support, the Ordinary can delegate any priest to consecrate it anew by the short formula prescribed by the Holy See.[19] Under Ordinary here come all those mentioned in can. 198, § 1, since the Code does not limit this power of delegation to the local Ordinary. A very short formula for this purpose was published by the S. Congregation of Rites, September 9, 1920.[20] This power granted here by the Code is new. It permits also major religious superiors of clerical exempt institutes to provide either through themselves or another priest for the consecration of an altar which has lost its consecration by the separation of the table from its support, although they can exercise this faculty only for their own churches. Before the Code, this power of reconsecrating an altar, desecrated as here indicated, was granted by the Holy See only by special request or concession, and not by law.[21]

2. The fixed altar is desecrated by a fracture which is regarded as very considerable by reason either of the break itself or of the anointed place.[22] A considerable fracture of the table of the altar (*fractura enormis*) was determined definitely as the cause of its desecration by Alexander III and Innocent III, and became the general law when incorporated by Gregory IX in his Decretals.[23] The Code has adopted the decision of the S. Congregation of Rites, given October 6, 1837,[24] in determining more specifically the nature of the fracture. Canonists and liturgists, however, do not agree on what constitutes an "enormous fracture." Some authors maintain that the fixed altar is not desecrated if a piece large enough to hold the chalice and paten

---

18 Coronata, *op. cit.*, p. 114; Vermeersch-Creusen, *Epitome*, II, n. 507.

19 Can. 1200, § 1.

20 *Acta Apost. Sedis*, XII (1920), 449. This formula is also found in the *Rituale Romanum* (Rome, 1925), appendix, tit. *De consecratione altarium exsecratorum* n. 1.

21 S. R. C., 28 Iul. 1883, *Decr. Auth.*, n. 3585.

22 Can. 1200, § 2, n. 1.

23 C. 1, 3, X, *de consecratione ecclesiæ vel altaris*, III, 40.

24 *Decr. Auth.*, n. 2777.

remains unbroken.[25] Gasparri designates this opinion as lax, and states rather the following general rule to determine the size of the break: *"Si in magno fragmento quod integrum remanet, reperiuntur omnes cruces ab episcopo in consecratione altaris specialiter benedictæ, fractura non est enormis; e contrario si in parvo fragmento reperitur aliqua ex his crucibus, fractura est enormis."*[26] The wording of the Code seems to favor this opinion. Consequently, a notable fracture would be:

a) If the table were broken in two or more large pieces, especially if the break in any way touched the relics [27], even if the parts are not fully separated from each other.[28]

b) If that portion of the table which the consecrator anointed is broken off.[29] Coronata, however, is of the opinion that the fixed altar is not desecrated if only one cross or place of unction is broken off, since it is not necessary for the validity to anoint all the crosses on the table of the altar.[30] The Code is explicit on the point and determines as a considerable break an anointed corner broken off, so that, it seems, it would not be safe to follow this opinion; for in the decree referred to by Coronata the S. Congregation of Rites prescribed all the anointings. If a small part of the corner is broken off, other than the place anointed, the altar is not desecrated.[31] In case of a doubt as to desecration concerning the size of the part broken off, it is left to the judgment of the bishop what is to be done.[32]

c) If several large stones of the support, adjacent to the table of the altar, were removed so that morally speaking, it could not be called the identical support.[33]

---

25 Reiffenstuel, *Ius Canonicum Universum,* lib. III, tit. 40, n. 37; Schmalzgrueber, *Ius Ecclesiasticum Universum,* lib. III, tit. 40, n. 43. Most of the authors in holding this opinion, it seems, have reference more to the portable altar than to the fixed altar.

26 *De SS. Eucharistia,* I, n. 340.

27 S. R. C., 23 Iun. 1879, *Decr. Auth.,* n. 3497.

28 S. R. C., *ibid.;* Blat, *Commentarium,* III (part 2), 65.

29 Can. 1200, § 2, n. 1; Gasparri *loc. cit.;* Schulte, *Consecranda,* p. 222; Vermeersch-Creusen, *Epitome,* II, n. 507; Woywod, "The Law of the Code on Altars," *The Homiletic and Pastoral Review,* XXVI (1925), 268-269.

30 *De Locis et Temporibus Sacris,* p. 115.

31 S. R. C., 3 Mart. 1821, *Decr. Auth.,* n. 2612; Gasparri, *op. cit.,* I, n. 340.

32 Reiffenstuel, *Ius Canonicum Universum,* lib. III, tit. 40, n. 37; Giraldi, *Expositio Iuris Pontificii,* Pars I, sec. 599; Many, *op. cit.,* p. 212; Prümmer, *Manuale Iuris Canonici,* p. 442.

33 Van der Stappen, *Sacra Liturgia,* III, 37; Schulte, *op cit.,* p. 222.

d) If one of the columns which support the table at the corners was removed, because the unction with the Holy Oils took place at the juncture of the table and support.[34]

3. The fixed altar is desecrated by the removal of the relics.[35] This was established by the universal practice of the Church requiring relics in the altar, as explained above. Among many of the older authors the desecration on account of removal of relics was not admitted, since they did not admit the necessity of relics for the validity of the consecration. This opinion, however, cannot be followed at the present day under any circumstances, since the Code is clear both in demanding the necessity of relics for the validity of the consecration and in declaring the altar desecrated if the relics are removed.[36]

No matter under what pretext the relics are removed, whether by chance or by design, the altar is desecrated by their removal, except in the case in which the bishop or his delegate causes a momentary removal of the relics for the purpose of fastening, repairing, or replacing the stone of the sepulchre or for the purpose of inspecting the relics themselves. The Code, it seems, allows only a momentary removal of the relics for inspection, to prove, for example, their genuineness. If the removal is not momentary, but endures for some time either from error or some other reason, even in the cases excepted, the altar is certainly desecrated.[37]

In like manner the fixed altar is desecrated in which relics have never been placed, except the case in which an altar is consecrated without relics by an apostolic indult. However, it is better to call such an altar invalidly consecrated, than to say it is desecrated.

4. The fixed altar is desecrated if the stone which covers the sepulchre for the relics is broken.[38] In this regard, however, the following considerations must be noted:

a) A slight break does not entail desecration of the altar, and any priest may fill the crack with cement, provided he does not remove the stone cover.[39] For making this repair, no delegation of the bishop or Ordinary is required.[40]

34 Van der Stappen, *loc. cit.;* Schulte, *loc. cit.*

35 Can. 1200, § 2, n. 2.

36 Coronata, *op. cit.*, p. 116; Many, *op. cit.*, p. 213.

37 Coronata, *op. cit.*, p. 116.

38 Can. 1200, § 2, n. 2.

39 Can. 1200, § 3.

40 An altar, whose stone cover of the sepulchre is found loose, but it is certain

b) If the break of the stone cover or lid of the sepulchre is made while the bishop or his delegate is removing it for the purpose of fastening it more securely, or repairing it, or substituting another, or even for inspecting the relics, the desecration of the altar is not caused thereby, because the Code allows the stone covering of the relics to be removed for the purposes named.[41]

c) The cement used to fasten more securely the stone cover of the sepulchre, or to repair it, or to substitute another, or to seal the sepulchre anew after an inspection of the relics, must be blessed according to the formula found in the Roman Pontifical.[42] This regulation must also be observed when it is done by a simple priest delegated by the bishop for this purpose.

5. Lastly, the fixed altar is desecrated by the removal of the stone cover of the sepulchre or cavity for the relics, except in the case when the bishop or his delegate removed it for the purpose of fastening, repairing, or replacing it, or for the purpose of inspecting the relics.[43] This regulation by which the altar is not desecrated if the stone cover of the sepulchre is removed by the bishop or his authority to inspect the relics, etc., is new. Before the Code, the contrary practice was in force, namely that the altar was desecrated by the removal of the stone cover even when done by the bishop to ascertain the authenticity of the relics, unless an apostolic indult had been obtained for this purpose.[44]

If a priest, without the proper delegation of the bishop, should remove the stone cover of the sepulchre, he would cause the altar to lose its consecration.[45] This faculty, by which the bishop can delegate a priest to perform a function reserved to the episcopal order is altogether new, at least in that general manner by which the Code grants it; nor can this faculty be used beyond the limits established by law.

---

it has not been removed, is not to be considered desecrated; before the Code the bishop himself was obliged to seal the sepulchre with new cement unless he had obtained an apostolic indult to delegate a simple priest. Since the Code, however, neither an apostolic indult nor the delegation of the bishop is required as is clearly stated in can. 1200, § 3. Cf. S. C. R., 18 Maii 1863, ad 10, *Decr. Auth.*, n. 3575.

41 Can. 1200, § 2, n. 2. Cf. Coronata, *op. cit.*, p. 117.

42 S. R. C., 3 Sept. 1879, ad 2, *Decr. Auth.*, n. 3504.

43 Can. 1200, § 2, n. 2.

44 Cf. S. R. C., 25 Sept. 1875, 14 Mart. 1861, *Decr. Auth.*, nn. 3379, 3106; Gasparri, *De SS. Eucharistia*, I, nn. 348 f.; Coronata, *op. cit.*, p. 117. Many, *Prælectiones de Locis Sacris*, p. 212.

45 S. R. C., 31 Aug. 1867, ad 5, *Decr. Auth.*, n. 3162.

In canon 1200, § 2, n. 2, the Code speaks of the delegate of the bishop; since under the name of the bishop are not included major religious superiors or vicars-general, or other ordinaries not bishops, these cannot make this inspection, or delegate any one for this purpose, although the bishop himself can delegate them or any other priest for this work.[46]

The formula to be used for reconsecrating an altar desecrated in any manner indicated in canon 1200, § 2, nn. 1-2, was published by the S. Congregation of Rites, September 9, 1920.[47]

III. The desecration of a church does not cause the desecration of either its fixed or portable altars, and vice versa.[48] The reason of this is that the consecration of the altar and the consecration of the church are two distinct consecrations and independent of each other. The Code in this regulation introduces nothing new in practice.[49]

IV. *Profanation or Violation of an Altar (Pollutio Altaris).* There is no special profanation or violation of an altar, distinct from the profanation or violation of a church. Consequently only indirectly is there a violation of an altar, for when a church is violated or profaned it carries with it the violation or profanation of all the altars constructed within it. Since an act of profanation or violation of a church causes the effects of the consecration or benediction to be suspended for the whole church, the consequence in reference to the altar is that Mass may not be celebrated on any altar of the church thus violated until the rite of reconciliation of the church has been performed. Once the reconciliation of the church has been accomplished by the formula prescribed in the Roman Ritual or the Roman Pontifical according as the church is blessed or consecrated, the altars may again be used for the celebration of Mass, for there is no special ceremony for reconciling the altars in a church that has been profaned or violated.[50]

---

46 Coronata, *De Locis et Temporibus Sacris,* pp. 113, 118.

47 *Acta Apost, Sedis,* XII (1920), 450 ff. This formula is also found in the *Rituale Romanum* (Rome, 1925), appendix, tit. *De consecratione altarium exsecratorum,* n. 2.

48 Can. 1200, § 4.

49 Cf. C. 1, X, *de consecratione ecclesiæ vel altaris,* III, 40; S. R. C., 3 Mart. 1821, *Decr. Auth.,* n. 2612; Coronata, *op. cit.,* p. 118; Gasparri, *op. cit.,* nn. 185, 346; Many, *op. cit.,* p. 213.

50 Cf. Reiffenstuel, *Ius Canonicum Universum,* lib. III, tit. 40, n. 36; Schmalzgrueber, *Ius Ecclesiasticum Universum,* lib. III, tit. 40, n. 47; Many, *Prælectiones de Locis Sacris,* p. 214; Coronata, *De Locis et Temporibus Sacris,* pp. 27, 118 f.

SECTION 2
THE PORTABLE ALTAR

CHAPTER I
THE CONSTRUCTION OF A PORTABLE ALTAR

§ 1. *Preliminary Remarks*

The portable or movable altar consists of a solid piece of natural stone, generally of small size, which alone is consecrated; or the same stone with its support, which was not consecrated together with the table as one whole.[1] The portable altar differs in many ways from the fixed altar. They differ first in size, for the stone-table of a fixed altar ordinarily covers the whole surface of the altar, while the portable altar, although it may be equally as large, is usually only large enough to hold the host and the chalice. Secondly, they differ in the manner of construction; for the stone-table of the fixed altar must be cemented to the support, whereas the portable altar is not necessarily joined by cement to its support, but can be moved from place to place and used wherever necessary. Thirdly, they differ in the location of the sepulchre for the relics; in the fixed altar four positions are allowed, three of which are in the support, but in the portable altar the sepulchre must be cut in the upper surface. Lastly, they differ in the manner of consecration, for in the consecration of the portable altar only the upper surface of the altar is anointed, whereas in the consecration of the fixed altar not only the upper surface is anointed with Chrism, but also the four corners are anointed at the conjunction of the table with the support so that not the altar-stone alone but the whole altar is considered consecrated.[2] This last difference, it may be said, constitutes the essential distinction between the fixed and the portable altar.

In this section the portable altar only is treated with all its require-

1 Can. 1197, § 1, n. 2. Cf. Part I, sec. 1, chap. iii.
2 De Herdt, *Praxis Sacræ Liturgiæ*, I, n. 176.

ments. Since it has many qualities in common with the fixed altar, to avoid unnecessary repetitions, references will be made to the preceding section for a full account of those details in common with all altars.

§ 2. *Material and Form*

1. *Material.* The portable altar must be of natural stone sufficiently hard to resist easy fracture. The stone itself must possess the same qualities as the table (*mensa*) of the fixed altar.[3] This is established:

a) From can. 1198, § 1. "*Tum mensa altaris immobilis tum petra sacra ex unico constent lapide naturali, integro et non friabili.*"

b) From the General Rubrics of the Roman Missal, c. XX: "*Altare . . . debet esse lapideum . . . . ., vel saltem ara lapidea, similiter ab episcopo vel abbate ut supra consecrata, in eo inserta, quæ tam ampla sit ut hostium et maiorem partem calicis capiat.*"

The portable altar, likewise, must be a single entire stone without any cracks or cavities. Only the sepulchre for the relics and the five small crosses, where the unctions are made, may be cut in it. A portable altar, composed of two or more stones cemented or joined together in any manner, may not be validly consecrated.[4]

2. *Form.* The portable altar may be square or oblong.[5] No special dimensions are prescribed for its size, but according to the Code[6] and the General Rubrics of the Roman Missal,[7] it must be large enough to hold the Sacred Host and the greater part of the base of the chalice. This is the minimum size. Most authors also maintain that it should be large enough to hold besides the Host and the chalice the ciborium, if the altar is intended for the celebration of Mass at which Holy Communion is distributed.[8] St. Charles Borromeo prescribed that

---

3 Cf. Part II, sec. 1, chap. i, § 2.

4 S. R. C., 19 Maii 1896, ad 3, *Decr. Auth.*, n. 3907.

5 Gasparri, *De SS. Eucharistia,* I, n. 302; Many, *Prælectiones de Locis Sacris,* p. 216; Schulte, *Consecranda,* p. 232; Martinucci-Menghini, *Manuale Sacrarum Cæremoniarum,* lib. VII, cap. 5, art. 1, § 1, n. 3.

6 Can. 1198, § 3.

7 C. XX, quoted above.

8 De Lugo, *De Sacramento Eucharistiæ,* Disput. XX, sec. 3, n. 69; Gasparri, *De SS. Eucharistia,* I, n. 292; Van der Stappen, *Sacra Liturgia,* III, 38; Schulte, *Consecranda,* p. 232; Coronata, *De Locis et Temporibus Sacris,* p. 107; De Herdt, *Sacræ Liturgiæ Praxis,* I, n. 176; Augustine, *A Commentary,* IV, 89.

the dimensions be 13¾ inches long and 11 inches wide.[9] In the archdiocese of Mechlin, the altar-stones are 14 inches square and about 2 inches thick. In general they may vary between 12 by 12 inches and 14 by 16 inches. Missionaries may use even smaller altar-stones than these described, because of the necessity of carrying them about from place to place on missionary journeys.[10]

The portable altar, however, may have larger dimensions than those stated above. It is especially fitting in churches which have no fixed altars, but only quasi-fixed or *ad modum fixi*, that the altar-stone be larger than those intended to be used on missionary journeys or for similar purposes. The altar-stone may also be as large as the structure upon which it rests; although it may be more prudent not to have the altar-stone such a size especially if the support is stone, since the altar then has the appearance of a fixed altar and may easily lead to error; for if the table becomes separated form the base, one would be justified in thinking the altar desecrated.[11]

Five small crosses are usually chiseled on the altar-stone or portable altar, one about two inches from each corner and one in the center to indicate the places at which the unctions are to be made in its consecration.[12] If, perchance, the cross in the center is wanting, the unction must not be omitted, although the omission of this unction would not invalidate the consecration.[13]

The altar-stone, or portable altar, after it has been properly consecrated, is placed upon a lower structure of sufficient height for the convenient celebration of Mass by the priest. This structure can be made of stone, metal, brick, wood, or any suitable or appropriate material; the table, in which the altar-stone is inserted, can also rest on columns. The whole must be so constructed that it has the ordinary appearance of an altar. The dimensions of this superficial structure should be the same as those of the fixed altar to enable the priest to move about correctly in accordance with the rubrics in the celebration of the Holy Sacrifice of the Mass. The altar-stone is inserted in the middle of the table of the altar about two inches from the front edge,

9 *Instructions on Ecclesiastical Building*, chap. XV, § 12.

10 Van der Stappen, *op. cit.*, III, 38-39; Schulte, *op. cit.*, pp. 232 f.

11 Van der Stappen, *op. cit.*, III, 39.

12 The chiseling of these crosses on the altar-stone is not required for the validity of the consecration, but is done principally to indicate the places where the unctions are made during the ceremonies of consecration.

13 S. R. C., 2 Maii 1892, *Decr. Auth.*, n. 3771; cf. Schulte, *op. cit.*, p. 233.

in such a manner that by its slight elevation above the table the celebrant can trace its outlines with his hand and thus recognize its position beneath the linen altar-cloths. In a blessed church it is fitting that at least one altar, particularly the high altar, be at least a quasi-fixed altar or *ad modum fixi,* namely an altar-stone or portable altar inserted in the lower structure in a permanent manner; this is important, for it is a sufficient condition for gaining the indulgence of a privileged altar.[14]

In a blessed church, all the altars can be portable or movable. In a consecrated church, the high altar should be a fixed altar, but all the other altars may be portable or movable.[15] This same regulation applies to public and semi-public oratories. In private oratories, however, only portable altars as described above can be erected.[16]

Moreover, what was said under the fixed altar about the prohibition to bury the dead near the altar or under the altar, applies with equal force in regard to the erection of portable altars or quasi-fixed altars.[17]

§ 3. The Sepulchre or Cavity for the Relics

1. *Nature of the Sepulchre for the Relics.* The sepulchre or cavity for the relics in the portable altar is a small opening made in the altar-stone, in which the relics are placed in its consecration according to the requirements of the liturgical laws.[18] This opening must be made on the top of the stone either toward its front edge or in the middle.[19] The reason of this is that the Roman Pontifical admits only four places for the location of the sepulchre for the relics, namely, one in the table of the altar and the other three in the support (*stipes*); as the three latter ways are incompatible with the portable altar, there remains only the manner of placing the relics in the altar-stone itself. Although the Roman Pontifical in this instance refers directly to the fixed altar, nevertheless the S. Congregation of Rites has extended this regulation to the portable altar.[20]

---

14 S. R. C., 31 Aug. 1867, ad 1, *Decr. Auth.,* n. 3162.
15 Can. 1197, § 2.
16 Cf. Coronata, *De Locis et Temporibus Sacris,* p. 109.
17 Cf. Part II, sec. 1, chap. i, § 6.
18 Can. 1198, § 4.
19 S. R. C., 31 Aug. 1867, ad 2, 31 Mart. 1887, *Decr. Auth.,* nn. 3162, 3671.
20 S. R. C., 31 Mart. 1887, ad 2, *Decr. Auth.,* n. 3671. Cf. Many, *Prælectiones de Locis Sacris,* p. 217.

No particular form is prescribed for the opening, but it must be suitably chiseled out, polished, and cleaned.[21] The usual form of the opening is square or oblong.[22] The S. Congregation of Rites declared as inadmissible a portable altar, consisting of two parts, the upper one of which was stone, whereas the lower was of wood, with a hollow space between both parts for the relics, which thus touched the stone and wooden parts forming the sepulchre.[23]

The sepulchre for the relics must not be made on the front edge of the altar-stone. The S. Congregation has decided this in several decrees.[24] Before the year 1880, many portable altars had been consecrated in this manner with the relics placed in the front edge of the altar stones, because it was found more convenient for transporting or carrying them from place to place. The question was placed before the S. Congregation of Rites whether altar-stones of this kind could be tolerated or should be changed and consecrated anew. The answer was given that as regards the portable altars already consecrated the bishop should not be disturbed,—"*Episcopus acquiescat;*" however, in the decision given June 13, 1899, the S. Congregation declared that where it could be conveniently done, altar-stones of this nature should be consecrated again by the short formula.[25] Consequently, in the light of these decisions, it seems that portable altars, having the sepulchre for the relics on the front edge, are invalidly consecrated, unless a special indult from the Holy See is obtained for this purpose.[26] Those altar-stones, which had been consecrated with the relics deposited in the manner described before the above decisions had been given, could be validly and licitly used for the celebration of Mass.[27]

2. *Stone cover of the Sepulchre (Operculum Sepulcri).* The cover or lid, used to seal the relics in the consecration of the portable altar,

---

21 Van der Stappen, *op cit.*, III, 40.
22 Augustine, *A Commentary*, VI, 90.
23 S. R. C., 31 Aug. 1867, ad 2, *Decr. Auth.*, n. 3162.
24 S. R. C., *Aequatorianæ Americæ*, 24 Nov. 1885, quoted by Many, *op. cit.*, p. 217, and *Ephemerides Liturgicæ*, I (1887), 348: "Quoad vero altaria quorum sepulcrum seu confessio non in medio altaris, sed in eius fronte fuit effosum ea non sunt admittenda, utpote Pontificalis Romani præscriptionibus haud conformis"; cf. S. R. C., 31 Mart. 1887, 13 Iun. 1899, *Decr. Auth.*, nn. 3671, 4032.
25 S. R. C., 13 Iun. 1899, ad 3, *Decr. Auth.*, n. 4032.
26 Cf. *Ephemerides Liturgicæ*, I (1887), 362-363.
27 *Ephemerides Liturgicæ, loc. cit.;* Van der Stappen, *Sacra Liturgia*, III, 42.

must be of natural stone, fitting exactly upon the opening.[28] This cover must be fastened with cement, blessed by the rite prescribed for the consecration of a fixed altar.[29] Hence, it is not sufficient to cover the sepulchre for the relics with wax, cement, or any similar material. In cases where the relics had been sealed with cement or other similar material only, the S. Congregation of Rites ordered the cement or other material than stone to be removed and the altar-stone to be consecrated anew; but allowed the short form of consecration to be used.[30] Metal likewise may not be used to cover the sepulchre; although if a metal cover is used, the consecration is not invalid for that reason.[31]

The episcopal seal, formed from wax or other material, can be placed upon the closed sepulchre, but this is not essential to the validity of the consecration;[32] whence it follows that the breaking or removal of this seal does not desecrate the altar-stone.[33] Moreover, since according to the requirement of placing the sepulchre for the relics on the top of the altar-stone, it is better not to attach the episcopal seal, because it can easily be rubbed off due to the friction from the altar-cloths and other causes.[34]

---

28 S. R. C., 31 Aug. 1867, ad 2, 15 Dec. 1882, ad 1, *Decr. Auth.*, nn. 3162, 3567.

29 S. R. C., 15 Dec. 1882, ad 2, 10 Maii 1890, ad 1, 21 Ian. 1898, ad 2, *Decr. Auth.*, nn. 3567, 3726, 3976.

30 S. R. C. 28 Iul. 1883, 30 Aug. 1901 *Decr. Auth.*, nn. 3585, 4082.

31 S. R. C., 23 Iun. 1892, ad 4, *Decr. Auth.*, n. 3779.

32 Gardellini, *Decreta Authentica,* Appendix V, n. 5803; S. R. C., 10 Maii 1890, ad 3, *Decr. Auth.*, n. 3726.

33 Schulte, *Consecranda,* p. 234.

34 Van der Stappen, *Sacra Liturgia,* III, 43.

CHAPTER II

THE CONSECRATION OF PORTABLE ALTARS

§ *1. The Necessity of Consecration*

In order that Mass may be celebrated on a portable altar or altar-stone, it is absolutely required that it be consecrated. This follows:

1. From can. 1199, § 1: *"Ut Missæ sacrificium super illud celebrari possit, altare debet esse, secundum liturgicas leges, consecratum; idest vel totum, si agatur de immobili, vel ara tantum portatilis, si de mobili."*

2. From the General Rubrics of the Roman Missal, c. XX: *"Altare ... debet esse lapideum ...., vel saltem ara lapidea, similiter ab episcopo vel abbate ut supra consecrata."*

What was said concerning the necessity of consecration of the fixed altar or of its doubtful consecration applies equally as well to the portable altar.[1]

§ *2. The Consecrating Minister*

Can. 1199, § 2. *"Aras portatiles, salvis peculiaribus privilegiis, omnes Episcopi consecrare possunt."*[2]

In canon 1199, § 2, the Code regulates the consecrator of portable altars. In accordance with the general principles of consecrations, the consecration of portable altars is reserved to bishops unless it is permitted to others by apostolic indult or by law;[3] but the Code recognizes also the special privileges or indults which the Holy See may have granted to priests to consecrate portable altars. These privileges remain intact.[4] Formerly in accordance with the regulations of the Council of Trent[5], the bishop of the diocese or another

1 Cf. Part II, sec. 1, chap. ii, § 1.

2 "Besides those especially privileged, all bishops may consecrate portable altars."—Augustine, *A Commentary*, VI, 92.

3 Can. 1149, § 1.

4 Can. 1199, § 2.

5 Sess. VI, *de reformatione*, c. 5.

bishop with his permission could validly and licitly consecrate portable altars; the bishop always validly consecrated altars, even without the permission of the Ordinary of the diocese.[6] The Code, however, extends the rights of the bishop in this matter so that he can validly and licitly consecrate altar-stones or portable altars even outside his territory without the permission of the bishop or other Ordinary of the place.

In accordance, therefore, with canon 1199, § 2, and other canons of the Code in which the privilege of consecrating portable altars is granted by law, the following may validly and licitly consecrate portable altars:

1. All bishops, whether residential or titular;[7]

2. All Cardinals, from the time of their promotion in the consistory to the cardinalate;[8]

3. Vicars and prefects apostolic, even if they do not enjoy the episcopal character, but only within the confines of their territory and during the tenure of office, provided they use the sacred oils consecrated by a bishop.[9] The pro-vicar or pro-prefect, or the senior priest of the vicariate or perfecture, who rules a vicariate or prefecture during its vacancy according to can. 309, enjoys this same faculty of consecrating altar-stones or portable altars as long as he holds office in this capacity.[10]

4. Abbots or prelates *nullius,* if they are not bishops, provided they have received the blessing if they must receive it. They can make use of this privilege, however, only within the confines of their own territory and during the tenure of their office, with the obligation likewise of using the sacred oils consecrated by a bishop.[11]

All others, who are not bishops and who are not mentioned above, but who nevertheless enjoy the right of consecrating portable altars, have it by apostolic indult or by special privilege. This privilege cannot be acquired either by prescription or by custom, even if im-

---

6 Many, *Prælectiones de Locis Sacris,* pp. 219 f.

7 Can. 1199, § 2.

8 Can. 239, § 1, n. 20.

9 Can. 294, § 2.

10 Can. 310. Cf. Paschang, *The Sacramentals,* p. 52; Winslow, *Vicars and Prefects Apostolic,* pp. 65 f.; Vermeersch-Creusen, *Epitome,* II, n. 506.

11 Can. 323, § 2.

memorial.[12] A bishop cannot grant to priests the faculty of consecrating altar-stones without special faculties from the Holy See. The Roman Pontiff, however, can grant this faculty, since it is a matter of ecclesiastical law. Many examples of this indult are found in the history of the Church. In the quinquennial faculties which the bishops or local Ordinaries usually obtain from the Holy See on the occasion of making the report on the state of their territory, they are granted authority to delegate priests, who, if possible, should be vested with an ecclesiastical dignity (as, for example, the vicar-general), to consecrate portable altars with the ceremonies described in the Roman Pontifical, or by merely using the approved shorter form of the Roman Ritual.[13]

§ 3. *Relics for the Portable Altar*

In the same manner that relics of saints or martyrs are prescribed for the fixed altar, they are necessary for the valid consecration of the portable altar.[14] The regulations pertaining thereto are the same as for the fixed altar; consequently, reference is made to what was said under this heading of the fixed altar for the full particulars and discussion of these regulations.[15] There is this difference, however, that in the consecration of the portable altar the relics of two martyrs[16] and three grains of incense are placed immediately, that is, without a reliquary, into the sepulchre; nor is it required to place an attestation of consecration together with the relics in the sepulchre, as is prescribed for the fixed altar.[17] The sepulchre for the relics is closed with a small piece of natural stone fitting exactly upon the opening. This cover, as has already been described, must be fastened with cement, blessed with the rite given for the consecration of a fixed altar.

---

12 Reiffenstuel, *Ius Canonicum Universum,* lib. III, tit. 40, n. 34; Gasparri, *De SS. Eucharistia,* I, n. 313; Many, *op. cit.,* p. 206; Coronata, *De Locis et Temporibus Sacris,* p. 112.

13 Cf. Vermeersch-Creusen, *Epitome,* II, appendix, n. 871.

14 "Tum in altari immobili tum in *petra sacra* sit, ad normam legum liturgicarum, sepulcrum continens *reliquias Sanctorum,* lapide clausum."—Can. 1198, § 4.

15 Cf. Part II, sec. 1, chap. ii, § 3.

16 The S. Congregation of Rites, February 16, 1906, declared that for the valid consecration of an altar, fixed or portable, it suffices to have inclosed in the sepulchre the relics of one martyr. Cf. S. R. C., 16 Febr. 1906, ad 3, *Decr. Auth.,* n. 4180.

17 Cf. Pontificale Rom., tit. *De altaris portatilis consecratione.*

§ 4. *The Ceremonies of Consecration*

The Roman Pontifical gives a special formula for the consecration of the portable altar [18], which must be observed in all particulars.[19] Consequently, it is not permitted in the consecration of portable altars to use the rite of consecration prescribed for the fixed altar; if, however, this rite is used for the portable altars, the consecration is valid, as can be deduced from the similarity of the ceremonies and prayers in both rites and from a decision of the S. Congregation of Rites, which declared that a portable altar, consecrated by the ceremonies of a fixed altar, was validly consecrated.[20] The consecration, therefore, of the portable altar differs little in substance from the consecration of the fixed altar; the difference consists mainly in this that there is no anointing of the support and that certain solemnities are lacking.

If several portable altars are consecrated at the same time, the formula for consecrating many portable altars should be used as it is found in the supplement to the appendix of the latest edition of the Roman Pontifical.[21]

If only one altar-stone is consecrated, the bishop himself cements and closes the sepulchre for the relics; if more than one are consecrated, he may be assisted by priests in closing the sepulchre for the relics. In this case the bishop spreads the cement over the ledge of the first sepulchre, then a priest closes this first sepulchre with the slab, and cements and closes the other sepulchres after the bishop has placed the relics and grains of incense within them.[22]

---

18 *Ibid.*

19 S. R. C., 22 Maii 1841, *Decr. Auth.*, n. 2826.

20 S. R. C., 17 Iun. 1843, ad 4, *Decr. Auth.*, n. 2862; cf. Many, *Prælectiones de Locis Sacris*, p. 220; Coronata, *op. cit.*, p. 111; Gasparri, *De SS. Eucharistia*, I, n. 314.

21 In the older editions of the Roman Pontifical, the rite of consecrating many portable altars at the same time was not given. The question was placed before the S. Congregation of Rites for solution as to what changes were to be made in the prayers and in the ceremonies when many portable altars had to be consecrated at the same time. The answer was given March 11, 1820, and is found in Gardellini, *Decreta Authentica*, n. 4565. This decision is not contained in the latest authentic collection of the S. Congregation, since the Pontifical in the latest edition has made ample provision for the consecration of many portable altars. Cf. Gasparri, *op. cit.*, I, n. 316.

22 Dubium II. An ipse Episcopus idem sepulcrum cæmento linire et lapide claudere debeat? Et S. R. C. reposuit ad II. "Si agatur de unico altari portatili consecranda, Affirmative; si vero agatur de pluribus Aris portatilibus consecrandis, satis est ut Episcopus liniat cæmento labium sepulcri

If the consecration of portable altars takes place on different days close together, the water, salt, ashes, and wine must be blessed on each day the consecration is performed; nor is it permitted to use the water blessed on the first day in the consecrations performed on the subsequent days.[23]

The relics to be placed in the altar-stones are not exposed the evening before the consecration as it is prescribed in the preparations for the consecration of the fixed altar. The relics must be prepared, however, in ample time for the consecration, and in the place where they are made ready, two candles should be kept burning before them. In a similar manner it is not prescribed to recite matins and lauds *De communi plurimorum martyrum* the evening before the consecration.

The consecration of the portable altar may take place on any day, during the morning hours. The ceremony may be performed in the church, the sacristy, or in any suitable place.[24] No fast is prescribed on the day preceding the consecration.

The remarks made under the ceremonies of consecration of the fixed altar as to the unctions with the Holy Oils and to a deficiency in the supply of the Sacred Oils apply equally as well in the consecration of portable altars.[25].

Instead of consecrating a fixed altar according to the rite prescribed for it, sometimes an altar, the table of which is a single stone, is consecrated according to the rite given for a portable altar. In this case, the altar remains only a portable altar. It has this advantage, that if it be accidentally, or by design removed from its support, it does not lose its consecration.[26] When an altar is consecrated in this manner, a declaration must be made clearly indicating that only the table *(mensa)* was consecrated in the manner of a portable altar so that if the table becomes separated from the base one is not deceived in thinking the altar is thereby desecrated.

---

unius Aræ, et dum ipse prosequitur in sacrarum Reliquiarum repositione, assistentes Sacerdotes lituram et cuiusque sepulcri clausuram peragant."—S. R. C., 10 Maii 1890, *Decr. Auth.*, n. 3726.

23 S. R. C., 9 Febr. 1867, *Decr. Auth.*, n. 3153.

24 Martinucci-Menghini, *Manuale Sacrarum Cæremoniarum*, lib. VII, tit. 2, cap. 5, art. 1, § 1, n. 4; Schulte, *Consecranda*, p. 232.

25 Cf. Part II, sec. 1, chap. ii, § 4, nn. 1-2.

26 Schulte, *op. cit.*, p. 269.

CHAPTER III.

THE DESECRATION OF THE PORTABLE ALTAR

The portable altar is desecrated in the same manner as the fixed altar is desecrated, except as regards the separation of the table from the support, which is applicable from its very nature only to the fixed altar. Before Mass may be celebrated upon a desecrated portable altar, it must be consecrated anew, unless the desecration was of such a nature that the stone could not be reconsecrated. The Code in can. 1200, § 2, nn. 2-4, designates the different cases in which the portable altar loses its consecration. In accordance with these regulations the portable altar becomes desecrated in the following ways:[1]

1. The portable altar is desecrated by a notable fracture by reason either of the size of the piece broken or of the place anointed.[2] A fracture is notable if the altar-stone is broken into two or more pieces, or if that corner of the altar-stone, which the consecrator anointed, is broken off.[3] The altar-stone is desecrated likewise if it is cracked in such a way as to separate it into two or more parts, provided the cracks extend through the entire stone, although the parts may not have come fully apart.[4]

2. The portable altar is desecrated by the removal of the relics, no matter under what pretext they may be moved whether by chance or by design; except in the case in which the bishop or his delegate causes a momentary removal of the relics for the purpose of fastening, repairing, or replacing the stone cover of the sepulchre, or for the purpose of inspecting the relics themselves.[5]

---

1 Since the desecration of the fixed and portable altars happens in the same manner, except for the case mentioned, reference is made to the preceding section under the heading of the "Desecration of the Fixed Altar" (Part II, sec. 1, chap. iii) for the discussion of the details pertaining thereto. In this chapter a summary with the essential details is given for the portable altar.

2 Can. 1200, § 2, n. 1.

3 Gasparri, *De SS. Eucharistia,* I, n. 340; Schulte, *Consecranda,* p. 270; Van der Stappen, *Sacra Liturgia,* III, 44.

4 S. R. C., 31 Aug. 1867, ad 3, *Decr. Auth.,* n. 3162; cf. Many, *Prælectiones de Locis Sacris,* p. 221.

5 Can. 1200, § 2, n. 2.

3. The portable altar is desecrated if the stone, which covers the sepulchre for the relics, is broken.[6] A slight break, however, does not entail desecration of the altar, and any priest may fill the crack with cement, provided he does not remove the stone cover.[7] If the stone which covers the sepulchre has merely become loose and has not been removed from its place, it may be fastened with new cement by any priest without special delegation from the bishop or Ordinary of the place. The cement must be blessed according to the formula found in the Roman Pontifical. If the break of the stone cover of the sepulchre is made while the bishop or his delegate is removing it for the purpose of fastening it more securely, or repairing it, or substituting another, or for inspecting the relics, the desecration of the altar-stone is not caused thereby, since the Code allows the stone cover of the sepulchre to be removed for the purposes named.

4. Finally, the portable altar is desecrated by the removal of the stone cover of the sepulchre or cavity for the relics, except in the case when the bishop or his delegate removes it for the purpose of fastening, repairing, or replacing it, or for the purpose of inspecting the relics.[8]

Portable altars, which have been desecrated in the manner indicated in Canon 1200, § 2, nn. 1-2, can be consecrated by the short formula published by the Holy See on September 9, 1920.[9]

The desecration of a church does not cause the desecration of the portable altars within it, and vice versa.[10]

---

6 Can. 1200, § 2, n. 2.

7 Can. 1200, § 3.

8 Can. 1200, § 2, n. 2.

9 *Acta Apost. Sedis,* XII (1920), 450 ff.; this formula is also found in the *Rituale Romanum* (Rome, 1925), appendix, tit. *De consecratione altarium exsecratorum,* n. 2.

10 Can. 1200, §4.

CHAPTER IV

THE PRIVILEGE OF A PORTABLE ALTAR

§ *1. Meaning and Extent of the Privilege*

The privilege of a portable altar is the privilege of celebrating Mass in any place, provided it be respectable and decent, upon a consecrated altar-stone. Celebration of Mass, however, at sea is excluded from this privilege.[1] The privilege, therefore, properly speaking, consists precisely in this that one is permitted to say Mass outside of a church and public or semi-public oratory, consecrated or blessed for divine worship. Besides the celebration of Mass at sea, Gasparri also excluded from this privilege the celebration of Mass in the open air or below the earth, because these places, even if properly fitted and clean, were not considered respectable and safe under the former legislation.[2] Since the publication of the Code, these restrictions seem to apply only to cases in which these places are expressly excluded by the indult granting the privilege of the portable altar, for the Code does not except these places by a positive law; consequently, only in cases, where the open air and subterranean places cease to be respectable and decent, would the privilege of the portable altar be excluded. There is no evident reason why in themselves the open air and subterranean places are not respectable and safe.[3]

The privilege of a portable altar, whether granted by law or by a special indult of the Holy See, is always personal, and is limited to the person to whom it is granted according to the words of the indult. Thus, for example, if the indult is granted to a lay person, no priest may celebrate Mass by virtue of that privilege except in the presence of the lay person to whom it was granted; but if he is present, any priest may celebrate Mass by virtue of the privilege of the portable

---

1 "Hoc privilegium (i.e., altaris portatilis) ita intelligendum est, ut secumferat facultatem ubique celebrandi, honesto tamen ac decenti loco et super petram sacram, non autem in mari."—Can. 822, § 3.

2 Gasparri, *De SS. Eucharistia,* I, n. 272; cf. Ojetti, *Synopsis Rerum Moralium,* I, n. 337.

3 Coronata, *De Locis et Temporibus Sacris,* p. 123; Augustine, *A Commentary,* IV, 172.

altar. If a priest has obtained the privilege of a portable altar, he cannot allow another priest to celebrate Mass by virtue of the indult, unless that be especially mentioned. Cardinals and bishops, however, enjoy special privileges in this regard, which will be considered later.[4]

Furthermore, the privilege of a portable altar must be distinguished from that of a private or domestic oratory. Although both privileges have much in common, they are not one and the same. The privilege of a private oratory refers primarily to the right of possessing or having a particular place reserved for divine services, whereas the privilege of a portable altar does not mean the right of possessing or having a portable altar, but carries with it the faculty of celebrating Mass in any suitable and becoming place on a consecrated altar-stone, mainly outside of a church or oratory consecrated or blessed for divine worship. Consequently, the principal differences between the privilege of a portable altar and that of a private oratory may be stated as follows:

1. The privilege of a portable altar includes the faculty of celebrating Mass not only in an unconsecrated or unblessed place, but also in a place not destined for divine worship; in the privilege of a private oratory, the place must be reserved only for divine worship and must be kept free from profane uses.[5]

2. The privilege of a private oratory absolutely excludes the faculty of celebrating Mass in bedrooms.[6] The privilege of a portable altar, it seems, does not exclude this faculty, unless the celebration of Mass in a bedroom is expressly forbidden in the indult granted by the Holy See. The clause forbidding the celebrating of Mass in a bedroom, mentioned in the Code[7], has reference to the permission granted *per modum actus* by the bishop or other Ordinary of the place to celebrate Mass on a portable altar outside of a church or oratory. If the Holy See, therefore, grants the privilege of a portable altar without this restrictive clause, a bedroom in itself is not excluded. However, if the bedroom is small, not ornate, or unbecoming for some other cause, it is excluded by force of the general law as a place not respectable and becoming for the celebration of Mass.

3. He who enjoys the privilege of a portable altar is not obliged to

---

4 Cf. Gasparri, *op. cit.*, I, n. 272; Coronata, *op. cit.*, p. 125.
5 Canons 822, § 3, 1196.
6 Can. 1196; cf. Coronata, *op. cit.*, pp. 79, 94, 124.
7 Can. 822, § 4.

have a visitation of the place by the Ordinary before he makes use of the privilege, whereas a private oratory must be inspected and approved by the Ordinary before Mass may be celebrated in it.[8]

4. Those, who assist at or hear Mass celebrated by a priest having the privilege of a portable altar, fulfill their obligation of attending Mass on Sundays and holydays of obligation. The only exception made by the Code to satisfy the obligation of hearing Mass is in private oratories, strictly domestic, unless this privilege is especially granted by the Holy See.[9]

§ 2. *Those who enjoy the Privilege of a Portable Altar*

The privilege of a portable altar is granted by law, or by an indult of the Holy See.[10] In the period before the Council of Trent, the Holy See was very generous in granting the privilege of the portable altar, as was shown under the history of the portable altar. Abuses, however, arose in the use of this privilege so that the Council of Trent in the decree "*Quanta Cura*" made strict regulations govering the celebration of Mass outside of a church or oratory, by means of which it indirectly revoked the privileges of a portable altar, which had been granted in the course of time. The privileges of Cardinals and bishops in this matter were exempted from this general revocation, as was declared frequently by papal documents and is admitted by all commentators.[11] After the Council of Trent the Holy See granted this privilege more sparingly. The Code, therefore, restates the discipline that has been observed since the above named decree; although it extends the privilege to many local Ordinaries.

The privilege of a portable altar is granted by law to the following:

1. All Cardinals, from the time of their promotion in the consistory; with the faculty likewise of permitting another Mass to be celebrated in their presence.[12] They also enjoy the privilege of celebrating Mass on the sea, using proper precautions.[13] In order that a

8 Cf. Can. 1195, § 1; Gasparri, *De SS. Eucharistia,* I, n. 272; Coronata, *De Locis et Temporibus Sacris,* p. 124.

9 Can. 1249; cf. Coronata, *loc. cit.*

10 "Privilegium *altaris portatilis* vel iure vel indulto Sedis Apostolicæ conceditur."—Can. 822, § 2.

11 Cf. Part I, sec. 2, chap. v; Benedict XIV, *De Sacrificio Missæ,* lib. III, cap. 6, nn. 1-5; Benedict XIV, ep. encycl. "*Magno cum,*" 2 Iun. 1751, § 2, *Fontes I. C.,* n. 413.

12 Can. 239, § 1, n. 7.

13 Can. 239, § 1, n. 8.

priest may celebrate the second Mass allowed by the above grant, the presence of the Cardinal himself is required; for the privilege is personal and has reference to the person of the Cardinal.[14] This was also the practice under the former legislation.[15] The faculty of celebrating aboard ship while traveling on the sea is granted under a special number, for it is not included in the general privilege of a portable altar.

2. All bishops, whether residential or titular, from the moment they receive official notification of their canonical provision; with the faculty likewise of permitting that another Mass be celebrated in their presence.[16] They also enjoy the privilege of celebrating Mass on board a vessel, provided all necessary precautions are taken to eliminate all dangers of irreverence; that is, the sea must be sufficiently calm and the place decent. Bishops enjoy this privilege in the same manner as Cardinals, and, consequently, are limited in the use of it as explained above. They may make use of this privilege outside their diocese without the permission of the diocesan bishop or other Ordinary of the place. In virtue of this privilege a bishop can allow only one priest to say Mass after he has celebrated, and at which he must be present; a third Mass can be permitted only if the place where the Mass is celebrated is the private oratory of the bishop. In the private oratory of the bishop, however, many Masses may be celebrated, whether the bishop is present or not, since a bishop's private oratory enjoys all the privileges of a semi-public oratory.[17] Those present at the Mass celebrated by virtue of the privilege of a portable altar, whether said by the bishop or by the priest as allowed in the case, fulfill their obligation of hearing Mass on Sunday or other holydays of precept, because the law regulating this obligation does not forbid the fulfilling of the precept under such circumstances [18] and because of a special sanction in this regard by the S. Congregation of Rites [19] which, it seems, is not abrogated by the Code.[20] The privilege of a portable altar is granted for the convenience and accommodation of Cardinals and bishops, so that they can make use of it

14 Coronata, *De Locis et Temporibus Sacris*, p. 125.
15 Gasparri, *De SS. Eucharistia*, I, nn. 263-267.
16 Can. 349, § 1, n. 1.
17 Can. 1198. The private oratory of a Cardinal enjoys this same privilege.
18 Can. 1249.
19 S. R. C., 22 Aug. 1818, 8 Iun. 1896, *Decr. Auth.*, nn. 2585, 3906.
20 Cappello, *De Sacramentis*, I, 621; Coronata, *op. cit.*, p. 126.

even when they are sick and cannot celebrate; for example, they can order a priest well-known to themselves to celebrate Mass on a portable altar *iuxta cubiculum suum,* suitably and ornately located.[21] Under the pre-Code legislation, the privilege of a portable altar for Cardinals and bishops was subject to several restrictions, as can be learned from various decisions of the Holy See narrated by Gasparri[22]; for example, it was not lawful for a bishop to go to a private home for the sole purpose of celebrating Mass. Although these restrictions may be recommended to be kept and the prudence of the bishop may dictate their general observance, they are no longer enjoined by the Code, since the Code is granting the privilege of the portable altar does not make mention of them.

3. Vicars and prefects apostolic also enjoy the privilege of a portable altar. If they are not bishops, they enjoy the privilege only during their term of office and within the confines of their territory.[23]

4. Administrators apostolic, unless their letters of appointment expressly rule otherwise.[24] If the administrator apostolic is not a bishop, he enjoys the privilege only as long as his term of office lasts and while he is within his territory.

5. Prothonotaries apostolic *de numero participantium.*[25] Prothonotaries apostolic *supranumerarii* and *ad instar* do not have the privilege

---

21 S. R. C., 12 Mart. 1836, *Decr. Auth.,* n. 2739; Gasparri, *op. cit.,* I, n. 270; Coronata, *loc. cit.*

22 *Op. cit.,* I, nn. 267-268.

23 Can. 308. Cappello, *De Sacramentis,* I, 621; Ayrinhac, *Constitution of the Church in the New Code of Canon Law,* p. 129; Coronata, *De Locis et Temporibus Sacris,* p. 126, but he assigns the reference to the wrong canon. It is not in virtue of can. 294, § 1, that vicars and prefects apostolic, who are not bishops, enjoy the privilege of a portable altar, but by can. 308, which grants them the privileges of prothonotaries apostolic *de numero participantium.* Cappello, *loc. cit.,* states that abbots and prelates *nullius* enjoy the privilege of a portable altar in virtue of can. 323. This canon does not entitle them to the privileges of bishops, although it imposes upon them the ordinary powers and obligations of a bishop. Since abbots and prelates *nullius* do not enjoy the privileges of bishops and the Code does not grant them an extension of privileges which include the privilege of a portable altar in the manner as vicars and prefects apostolic have it, it must be concluded that abbots and prelates *nullius* do not have the privilege of a portable altar by law.

24 Can. 314, 315.

25 Pius X, motu proprio, *"Inter Multiplices,"* 21 Febr. 1905, nn. 2, 11; Pius IX, const. *"Quamvis peculiaris,"* 9 Febr. 1853: "Insuper Protonotariis participantibus privilegium Altaris portatilis ratum habemus ac confirmamus ea tamen lege ac conditione, ut illud in alienæ habitationis domibus erigere numquam possint nisi ipsi occasione itineris, seu hospitii gratia in iisdem domibus diversentur, utque Missa, quam super idem altare decenti

of a portable altar, although they enjoy the privilege of a private oratory.[26]

6. Auditors of the Holy Roman Rota enjoy the privilege of a portable altar in virtue of which they may celebrate Mass upon it in places appropriate and becoming for this purpose, provided the rights of others are safeguarded. Those present can fulfill the obligation of a preceptive Mass.[27]

All other privileges of a portable altar are held in virtue of a special indult from the Holy See. Those who enjoy the privilege by a personal concession must observe the conditions under which it is granted. Ordinarily the celebration of Mass by only one priest is permitted. No day, as a rule, is excepted besides the last three days of Holy Week; wherefore the privilege of a portable altar may be used on those days when the celebration of Mass is prohibited in private oratories.[28] Any cleric or lay person may obtain the privilege of a portable altar by special concession; in this case the privilege implies the permission of hearing Mass celebrated by any priest on a portable altar, in a respectable and decent place chosen by the one having the indult.

Priests in missionary countries are usually granted the privilege of a portable altar, generally with certain restrictions. They obtain this privilege either directly from the Holy See or indirectly from the bishops or other local Ordinaries; for the S. Congregation for the Propagation of the Faith is accustomed to grant to local Ordinaries in missionary countries the faculty of communicating this privilege to their missionaries. In these circumstances it is usually granted

---

semper in loco erigendum diebus etiam solemnioribus vel per se celebraverint vel per alium Sacerdotem sæcularem seu regularem rite probatum celebrari fecerint, tum Protonotariis ipsis eorumque consanguineis et affinibus cohabitantibus, tum personis eorum famulatui seu comitatui addictis, nunquam vero aliis personis in Ecclesiastici præcepti implementum suffragetur."—*Ex Actibus Pii IX,* I, 413-414. Cf. Cappello, *loc. cit.;* Ayrinhac, *loc. cit.*

26 Pius X, motu propr. *"Inter Multiplices,"* 21 Febr. 1905, nn. 22, 46; S. R. C., *Decr. Auth.,* n. 4154.

27 "Ius habent altaris portatilis et oratorii privati cum faculate Missam celebrandi ante diluculum et per horam post meridiem quod Missæ Sacrificium valeat etiam in præcepti adimplementum."—Wernz, *Ius Decretalium,* V, n. 85, footnote 53, n. 6; cf. Gasparri, *De SS. Eucharistia,* I, n. 271; Many, *Prælectiones de Missa,* p. 17; Cappello, *De Sacramentis,* I, 621; Coronata, *De Locis et Temporibus Sacris,* p. 127.

28 Cappello, *loc. cit.*

for cases of necessity or for conditions in which there is no other way of celebrating.[29]

Before the Council of Trent nearly all regulars enjoyed the privilege of a portable altar either directly by apostolic indult or indirectly through the communication of privileges.[30] This privilege was abrogated by the Council of Trent[31], as all authors admit.[32] In order to enjoy this privilege after the Council of Trent, they had to obtain it anew, or otherwise fall under the common law prohibiting Mass outside of churches or oratories consecrated or blessed for divine worship. However, many religious orders have obtained this privilege, usually with special limitations, from the Holy See; as, for example, the Canons Regular of the Lateran from Pius IV, March 8, 1565; the Fathers of the Society of Jesus from Gregory XIII, October 1, 1579, for their missions and with certain restrictions; the Friars of the Order of Preachers from Gregory XIII, June 20, 1580, for the province of Poland.[33]

Finally, the local Ordinary, or in the case of an exempt religious house, the major superior, may grant permission for a just and reasonable cause to say Mass outside a church or oratory, upon a consecrated altar-stone, provided the place is respectable and is not a bedroom, for extraordinary cases only and not habitually.[34] The major religious superiors who may grant this permission are those mentioned in can. 488, n. 8; namely, the abbot primate, abbots who are superiors of monastic congregations, abbots of monasteries that are independent although belonging to some monastic congregation, the superior general of any religious organization, the provincial superiors and their vicars, and all who have the same jurisdiction as provincials. A major superior of exempt religious, however, can give the permission in question only with regard to a house of his own religious institute. Hence, without a special indult he cannot permit his subjects to say Mass in a strange place not owned or controlled by the religious, for instance, while the religious is on a missionary journey.

---

29 Cf. Vermeersch-Creusen, *Epitome*, I, appendix II, n. 814, where the present formula of faculties granted by the Propoganda is found.

30 Gattico, *De Usu Altaris Portatilis*, cap. 8, nn. 1 ff.; Gasparri, *De SS. Eucharistia*, I, n. 262; Many, *Prælectiones de Missa*, p. 14.

31 Sess. XXII, decr. *de observandis et evitandis in celebratione missæ.*

32 Gattico, *op. cit.*, cap. 13; Gasparri, *loc. cit.;* Many, *loc. cit.*

33 Gattico, *op. cit.*, cap. 13, nn. 13 ff.; Gasparri, *loc. cit.;* Many, *op. cit.*, p. 16.

34 Can. 822, § 4.

In this case the competent Ordinary is the Ordinary in whose territory the religious wishes to say Mass.[35] The local Ordinary is the one commissioned to watch over his diocese, and is responsible for abuses which may creep in. He (and the major superior of exempt religious for cases under his control) may grant the permission in question under the following conditions:

1.° That Mass be said on a consecrated altar-stone (portable altar);

2.° That the place in which Mass is to be celebrated is respectable and becoming. Decency here must be judged not only by adornment, but also by the respect and reverence due the august Sacrifice. Bedrooms are also excluded as not being suitable places, nor can the Ordinary give permission to celebrate in them. It is forbidden to say Mass in the churches of heretics and schismatics.[36] The open air is considered a becoming place, when necessity demands that it be used. Proper precaution must be taken in such circumstances that all dangers from the wind, storms, or the elements be obviated.

3.° That the permission be granted for a just and reasonable cause. The following are considered reasonable causes: if the church or oratory in the place could not hold all the people on some special feast day or celebration; if an epidemic, raging in a town or city, necessitated the closing of churches; if all the churches or oratories in the territory were destroyed by fire or earthquake; however, if only one church was destroyed, and there were other churches to which the faithful could go, this would not be sufficient reason, unless the other churches would be at too great a distance; if there were no church or oratory in the place, to enable the faithful to hear Mass, as, for example, in missionary districts of large dioceses; if the precept of receiving the Easter Communion could not otherwise be complied with; if the administration of the Viaticum required it; if the military camps are too distant from the church or public oratory; for the benefit of sailors, who cannot go to a church, Mass may be celebrated near the sea-shore with proper precautions, provided the place is respectable.[37]

---

35 S. C. de Prop. Fide, 18 Nov. 1765, *Collectanea,* n. 461; cf. Augustine, *A Commentary,* IV, 171.

36 Can. 823, § 1.

37 Gasparri, *De SS. Eucharistia,* I, n. 276; Gattico, *De Usu Altaris Portatilis,* cap. 10, nn. 2-27; Many, *Prælectiones de Missa,* pp. 11 f.; Ver-

4.° The permission, however, is not to be granted as an habitual faculty or a right which the priest may employ at his pleasure, but only as the text of the Code says, *in casu extraordinario et per modum actus*. This implies that a priest must ask for it every time he had to celebrate outside of sacred places. The permission may be granted so as to allow Mass to be said in private houses on any day permitted by the general rubrics of the Roman Missal, provided the circumstances required are verified. The Ordinary, however, must issue this permission gratis.[38] Finally, the Commission for the Interpretation of the Code answered that the faculty granted to the Ordinary in can. 822, § 4, must be strictly interpreted.[39]

---

meersch-Creusen, *Epitome*, II, n. 100; Augustine, *A Commentary*, IV, 172; Petra, *Commentaria ad Constitutiones Apostolicas*, IV, 151.

38 S. C. de Sacramentis, 22 Mart. 1915, ad 1, *Acta Apost. Sedis*, IV (1912), 725.

39 *Acta Apost. Sedis*, XI (1919), 478; cf. S. C. de Sacramentis, *Litterae ad Rev.mos Ordinarios Italiae*, 26 Iul. 1924, *Acta Apost. Sedis*, XVI (1924), 370-371.

PART III

MISCELLANEA

CHAPTER I

THE TITLE OF AN ALTAR

§ *1. The Fixed Altar*

1. *Meaning and Necessity.* The title of an altar is the saint or mystery in whose honor or name the altar is erected or dedicated and by which it is known and distinguished from others.[1]

In the same manner as the church has its title, so also all the altars of a church, at least those that are fixed, must have their proper title.[2] This canon imposes the strict obligation of choosing a title for every fixed altar. However, this obligation in no manner affects the validity of the consecration of the altar, so that if the altar is consecrated without a particular title, the consecration of the church or altar is valid. The title is bestowed in the consecration of the church or the altar, for the Roman Pontifical prescribes that the name or names chosen be mentioned in several places in the ceremonies of consecration.[3] The bishop or other Ordinary of the place chooses the title of the altar; or the choice of the title may be made by the patron or by others interested in the building of the church or altar with the consent of the local Ordinary.[4]

2. *Titles to be Chosen.* The choice of a title of an altar is governed by the same general regulations as the title of a church. Consequently, the following titles may be chosen for an altar.[5]

---

1 Gasparri, *De SS. Eucharistia,* I, n. 306; Many, *Prælectiones de Locis Sacris,* pp. 52, 225.

2 "Sicut ecclesia, ita quodlibet etiam ecclesiæ altare, saltem immobile, proprium sibi titulum habeat."—Can. 1201, § 1.

3 Cf. Pontificale Rom., tit. *De ecclesiæ dedicatione seu consecratione,* tit. *De altaris consecratione quæ fit sine ecclesiæ dedicatione.*

4 Coronata, *De Locis Temporibus Sacris,* p. 120.

5 Cf. Gasparri, *op. cit.,* I, nn. 306, 138; Many, *op. cit.,* pp. 53, 225; Coronata, *op. cit.,* p. 120.

a) The Holy Trinity, or one of the divine persons;

b) Christ, our Lord, or one of the mysteries pertaining to Him, as, for example, the Incarnation, Nativity, Transfiguration, or any sacred object which has had any relation to His life, as, for example, the cross, the crown of thorns;

c) The Blessed Virgin Mary, or any of her special mysteries or prerogatives;

d) The Angels, whose names are known; namely, Michael, Gabriel, and Raphael; or the Holy Angels collectively, or the Holy Guardian Angels;

e) Any Saint, whose name is found in the Roman Martyrology or the Catalogue of Saints; or some fact, worthy of special memory, pertaining to the saint, as, for example, the Conversion of St. Paul, and the Stigmata of St. Francis.

Without the permission of the Apostolic See, altars may not be dedicated to the Blessed, even in churches and oratories which have received permission to say Mass and Office in their honor.[6]

The principal title of the high altar must be the same as the title of the church.[7] By the use of the expression *titulus primarius,* the Code permits the altar to have several titles in the same manner as churches; in this case all the titles except the principal one are con-titular. Moreover, in the same church no two altars can have the same title;[8] although several altars may be erected in honor of our Lord and the Blessed Virgin in the same church, provided they are dedicated under different titles.[9]

The title of the altar as such is not celebrated by the same rite as the title of the church. Consequently if the titular feast is not celebrated in the calendar of the diocese or of the church, Mass cannot be celebrated in honor of the feast except as a votive Mass in accordance with the general rubrics for such Masses or by a special indult of the Holy See.[10]

3. *Change of Title.* The title of a fixed altar cannot be changed without special permission of the Holy See.[11]

---

6 Can. 1201, § 4.
7 Can. 1201, § 2.
8 Gasparri, *op. cit.,* I, n. 306; Coronata, *op. cit.,* p. 120.
9 Ojetti, *Synopsis Rerum Moralium,* I, n. 331.
10 Many, *op. cit.,* p. 226; Gasparri, *loc. cit.;* Coronata, *loc. cit.*
11 Can. 1201, § 3.

§ 2. *The Portable Altar*

Portable or movable altars should also have a title in honor of some saint, mystery, or sacred thing in the same manner as fixed altars. The obligation of giving a title to a portable altar is not as great as that of giving a title to the fixed altar, since the Code in can. 1201, § 1, uses the expression that at least every fixed or immovable altar (*saltem immobile*) must have its own title. For portable altars, therefore, the obligation is one of suitableness and propriety.[12] The reason of this seems to be because the title is not given to the portable altar in its consecration, but is bestowed upon it when it is erected into a quasi-fixed altar. Portable altars, which are used strictly as such, that is, which are used on missionary journeys or are moved from place to place, are given no special title.

The title of a portable altar or quasi-fixed altar is governed by the same regulations as those pertaining to the fixed altar. However, with the permission of the Ordinary, which here includes the major superior of a clerical exempt institute, the title of a portable or quasi-fixed altar may be changed.[13]

---

12 Coronata, *op. cit.*, p. 119.
13 Can. 1201, § 3.

CHAPTER II

THE PRIVILEGED ALTAR

1. *Definition.* An altar is said to be privileged when, in addition to the ordinary fruits of the Eucharistic Sacrifice, a plenary indulgence is also granted whenever Mass is celebrated thereon. Wherefore, the privilege of this kind of an altar consists in a plenary indulgence, which, as far as the intention of the Supreme Pontiff and the use of the power of the keys extend, is sufficient in itself to free forthwith a soul from the pains of purgatory; but as far as the efficacy of the application is concerned, it is an indulgence the measure of which must be left to the divine mercy and acceptance.[1] From this it is evident that the effect of this indulgence is not infallible; for, although the Roman Pontiff offers to God from the treasury of the Church in as far as it is sufficient to liberate a soul immediately from the pains of purgatory, God is not bound to accept this price, and hence the acceptance or the measure of the acceptance depends on the mercy of God.[2] For this reason the Church has permitted anniversary and foundation Masses to be celebrated indefinitely on a privileged altar [3], and it has been the practice in the Church to celebrate Mass repeatedly on a privileged altar for the same deceased person.[4]

There are also altars which are privileged for the living, or for the living and the dead. Such altars today are a great exception, and they are rarely found outside of Rome. The privileged altar for the living usually meant that the faithful could gain either a plenary or partial indulgence by making a visit to such an altar,—the indulgence to be applied either for the living or for the dead according to the indult. However, where the inscription, *altare privilegiatum pro vivis atque defunctis,* was found on altars without any

---

[1] S. C. Indulg., 28 Iul. 1840, *Decr. Auth.,* n. 283.

[2] Cappello, *De Sacramentis,* I, 623.

[3] S. Pœnit. (Sect. de Indulg.), 6 Iul. 1917, ad 2, *Acta Apost. Sedis,* IX (1917), 440. Formerly, it was forbidden to receive perpetual Masses to be said on a privileged altar. Cf. S. C. Indulg., 16 Nov. 1711, *Decr. Auth.,* n. 41.

[4] Noldin, *De Sacramentis,* p. 375.

further restriction, the Holy See delared that this must be interpreted to mean that a plenary indulgence is granted as well for the living if the Mass is offered for the living as for the dead if the Mass is offered for the dead; for the living by way of jurisdiction, but for the dead by way of suffrage.[5] Since at the present time privileged altars are almost exclusively granted for the dead, only such altars will be treated in this chapter.[6]

2. *Division.* The privileged altar is of two kinds, local or real, and personal:

a) Local or real, when the privilege is annexed to the altar itself, and hence every priest who celebrates Mass at such an altar enjoys the privilege.

b) Personal, when the privilege is granted to a priest, so that it does not depend upon a certain altar, but on the priest who celebrates. Hence on whatever altar he celebrates, whether it be fixed or portable, and in whatever church or oratory he celebrates, the altar he uses is for the time being a privileged altar.

The real privileged altar is distinguished into *perpetual,* which continues indefinitely, and *temporary,* which is granted for a definite length of time, as, for example, for seven years. The personal privileged altar is also granted either *for perpetual use,* or *for a certain length of time,* or *for every day,* or *for certain days in a week.*

3. *The Construction of the Privileged Altar.* The privileged altar, when real or local, must be a fixed or immovable altar, but in a broad sense; that is, it must be stationary or permanent, either built on a solid foundation or attached to a wall or column, even though the structure as a whole is not consecrated, but has merely a consecrated altar-stone (portable altar) inserted in its table. It is not required that the altar be fixed or immovable in the strict liturgical sense of canon 1197, § 1, n. 1, but that it be *ad modum fixi,* as the S. Congregation of Indulgences declared in a decision given on March 20, 1846, and subsequently repeated in similar decisions.[7] The privilege is annexed not to the altar-stone, but to the structure itself by reason of the title which it bears, that is, of the mystery or saint

5 S. C. Indulg., 25 Aug. 1897, ad 3, *Acta Sanctæ Sedis,* XXX, 278-279.

6 Cf. Beringer-Steinen, *Die Ablässe, ihr Wesen und Gebrauch,* pp. 529-530.

7 S. C. Indulg., 20 Mart. 1846, *Decr. Auth.,* n. 334; Schneider, *Rescripta Authentica S. C. Indulg.,* 26 Mart. 1867, n. 405; S. C. Indulg., 18 Iul. 1902, ad 2, 3, *Acta Sanctæ Sedis,* XXXV, 62.

to whom it is dedicated. Hence if the material of the altar is changed, if the altar is transferred to another place within the same church, or if another altar be substituted for it in the same church, provided it retains the same title, the privilege is preserved.[8] However, if the altar to which the privilege is attached is destroyed and is erected again under a different title, the privilege is lost.[9] When a privileged altar is destroyed, the privilege is lost; but it revives if the altar is restored within fifty years and is erected under the same title in the same church.[10]

In order to indicate the fact that an altar is privileged, an inscription should be placed upon it in a spot easily seen by the priest or prelate celebrating Mass upon it. The only inscription necessary for this purpose is *altare privilegiatum,* whether the privilege is perpetual or for a certain time, daily or not, according to the wording of the grant.[11]

4. *Altars which are privileged.* Every altar is privileged by law throughout the universal Church as follows:

a) On All Souls' Day, all Masses enjoy the same privileges as if they were said on a privileged altar;[12]

b) All the altars of a church are privileged on the days when the Forty Hours' Devotion is held.[13]

Bishops, abbots or prelates *nullius,* vicars and prefects apostolic, and the major superiors of clerical exempt institutes may designate and declare one altar daily privileged forever in their cathedral, abbatial, collegiate, conventual, parochial, or quasi-parochial churches, provided there be no privileged altar already present in the churches named.[14] The vicar-general or vicar-capitular is not included, and may not designate a privileged altar.[15] Privileged altars may not be designated by the foregoing prelates or Ordinaries in public or semipublic oratories, except when such an oratory is united to the parish church or serves as a subsidiary to it.[16]

---

8 S. C. Indulg., 16 Sept. 1723, 24 Apr. 1843, *Decr. Auth.,* nn. 84, 317.
9 S. C. Indulg., 18 Iul. 1712, *Decr. Auth.,* n. 43.
10 Canons, 75, 924, § 1.
11 Can. 918, § 1.
12 Can. 917, § 1.
13 Can. 917, § 2.
14 Can. 916.
15 Augustine, *A Commentary,* IV, 366; Cappello, *De Sacramentis,* I, 625; cf. S. C. Indulg., 24 Maii 1843, *Decr. Auth.,* n. 321.
16 Can. 916.

The personal daily privileged altar is granted by the Code to the following persons:

a) All Cardinals from the time of their promotion in the consistory;[17]

b) All bishops, whether residential or titular, from the time of their receiving authentic notification of the canonical promotion.[18]

All priests, who have made the heroic act of charity in offering all their prayers and good works by way of suffrage for the poor souls in purgatory, enjoy by a special indult the personal privilege of a daily privileged altar.[19]

All others enjoy the right of a privileged altar by special indult of the Holy See. Such indults granted before the Code retain their full value.[20] Moreover, by belonging to certain societies, the grant of a privileged altar may be obtained under certain conditions and restrictions, usually for a certain number of days in each week.

5. *Conditions for gaining the Indulgence.* The indulgence of a privileged altar is granted in favor of the soul for which the Mass is offered. Hence, the Mass and the indulgence cannot be divided, but must be applied together for the same deceased person.[21] Consequently, if the Mass is celebrated for one deceased person, the indulgence and the fruits of the Mass must be applied for him; but if the Mass is celebrated for many deceased persons or for the poor souls in general, the indulgence of the privileged altar should be limited to one of them, previously determined by the celebrant of the Mass, as the Holy See has repeatedly decided.[22] If the Mass is offered both for the living and for the dead, the indulgence of the privileged altar cannot be applied to the soul of one deceased person; nor can the indulgence be gained if the Mass is offered for the living, unless it is an altar which is privileged both for the living and the dead, as was explained above.

In order to gain the indulgence of a privileged altar, the priest

---

17 Can. 239, § 1, n. 10.

18 Can. 349, § 1.

19 S. C. Indulg., 19 Nov. 1854, Schneider, *Rescripta Auth.*, n. 392.

20 Can. 4.

21 S. C. Indulg., 19 Dec. 1885, ad 5, 25 Aug. 1897, ad 1, *Acta Sanctæ Sedis*, XVIII, 339, XXX, 278-279.

22 S. C. Indulg., 29 Febr. 1864, ad 1, 19 Iun. 1880, ad 2, *Decr. Auth.*, nn. 402, 451; S. Pœnit. (Sect. de Indulg.), 6 Iul. 1917, ad 1, *Acta Apost. Sedis*, IX (1917), 440.

under the present legislation of the Church is not obliged to say the *Missa de Requiem* or to add the special prayer for the dead in the ferial Mass or Mass of a vigil, as was formerly required; nevertheless, the Holy See declared it to be fitting and proper that the votive Mass for the dead, or the ferial Mass or Mass of the vigil with the prayer for the deceased person, be said when the rubrics of the Missal permit it.[23]

6. *Gregorian Altar.* This name is given to the altar of St. Gregory in the church of the same title on the Cælian Hill of Rome. The custom has prevailed from ancient times to the present day for the faithful to ask that the Holy Sacrifice of the Mass be offered for the dead on this special altar of St. Gregory in Rome with the pious thought that every Mass offered on this altar has such efficacy that the soul for which it is offered is freed forthwith from the pains of purgatory. The S. Congregation of Indulgences has called this confidence, pious and approved in the Church.[24] The same privilege which is proper to the altar of St. Gregory has been extended to other altars, which are called Gregorian Altars *ad instar*.[25] The Holy See published a decree December 12, 1912, in which it was declared that the Altar of St. Gregory on the Cælian Hill in Rome is truly and properly a privileged altar, and that from the time of the decree no privileges of a Gregorian Altar *ad instar*, were to be granted.[26] The altar of St. Gregory, or the Gregorian Altar *ad instar*, therefore, is an altar so privileged that there are two concessions which contribute to make more certain the application of the indulgence, namely, the authority of the Church and the intercession of St. Gregory, by which through the Holy Sacrifice of the Mass offered on this altar souls may be freed from the pains of purgatory.[27]

---

23 S. C. S. Off. (Sect. de Indulg.), 20 Febr. 1913, *Acta Apost. Sedis*, V (1913), 122.

24 S. C. Indulg., 11 Mart. 1884, ad 2, *Collectanea S. C. de Prop. Fide*, II, n. 1613.

25 For example, the high altar of the crypt of St. Benedict, at Montecassino, Italy; cf. *Acta Apost. Sedis*, V (1913), 115.

26 S. C. S. Off. (Sect. de Indulg.), 12 Dec. 1912, ad 6, 7, *Acta Apost. Sedis*, V (1913), 33.

27 Cf. *Ephemerides Liturgicæ*, XXX (1916) 363; Noldin, *De Sacramentis*, pp. 377 f.

Universitas Catholica Americae

Washingtonii, D. C.

Facultas Iuris Canonici

1926-1927

No. 38

TITULI

DEUS LUX MEA

TITULI

QUOS

AD DOCTORATUS GRADUM

IN

IURE CANONICO

APUD UNIVERSITATEM CATHOLICAM AMERICÆ

CONSEQUENDUM

PUBLICE PROPUGNABIT

NICOLAUS MARTINUS BLILEY, O. S. B.,

SACERDOS ABBATIÆ NULLIUS BELMONTANÆ

IURIS CANONICI LICENTIATUS

HORA XI A. M. DIE XXIII MAII A. D. MCMXXVII

De Iure Publico Ecclesiastico

I. De Forma Regiminis in Ecclesia.
II. De Relatione inter Ecclesiam et Statum.
III. De Concordatis in Genere.

De Iure Canonico

IV. De Fontibus Iuris Canonici.
V. De Codificatione Novi Codicis.
VI. Canones 1-86. Normæ Generales.
VII. Canones 90-95. De Domicilio et Quasi-domicilio.
VIII. Canon 98. De Personis quoad Ritum.
IX. Canones 111-117. De Clericorum adscriptione alicui diœcesi.
X. Canones 222-229. De Concilio Oecumenico.
XI. Canones 319-328. De Prælatis Inferioribus.
XII. Canones 329-332. De Nominatione et Institutione Episcopi.
XIII. Canones 334-336. De Officiis et Obligationibus Episcopi.
XIV. Canon 338. De Obligatione Episcopi quoad Residentiam.
XV. Canon 349. De Privilegiis Episcopi.
XVI. Canones 366-371. De Vicario Generali.
XVII. Canones 451-454. De Officio Parochi.
XVIII. Canon 466. De Obligatione Parochi quoad Missam pro Populo.
XIX. Canones 492-498. De Erectione et Suppressione Religionis, Provinciæ, Domus.
XX. Canones 518-530. De Confessariis et Cappellanis.
XXI. Canones 542-552. De requisitis ut Quis in Novitiatum admittatur.
XXII. Canones 572-586. De Professione Religiosa.
XXIII. Canones 632-636. De Transitu ad aliam Religionem.
XXIV. Canones 738-744. De Ministro Baptismi.
XXV. Canones 780-800. De Sacramento Confirmationis.
XXVI. Canones 802-813. De Sacerdote Missæ Sacrificium celebrante.
XXVII. Canones 893-900. De Reservatione Peccatorum.
XXVIII. Canones 1019-1034. De iis quæ Matrimonii celebratione præmitti debent et præsertim de Publicationibus Matrimonialibus.
XXIX. Canones 1058-1066. De Impedimentis Impedientibus.
XXX. Canones 1094-1103. De Forma Celebrationis Matrimonii.
XXXI. Canones 1118-1132. De Separatione Coniugum.
XXXII. Canones 1197-1202. De Altaribus.
XXXIII. Canones 1250-1254. De Abstinentia et Ieiunio.
XXXIV. Canones 1395-1405. De Prohibitione Librorum.
XXXV. Canones 1556-1568. De Foro Competenti.
XXXVI. Canones 1960-1992. De Causis Matrimonialibus.
XXXVII. Canones 2147-2156. De Modo procedendi in Remotione Parochorum inamovibilium.
XXXVIII. Canones 2215-2219. De Pœnarum Notione, Speciebus, Interpretatione atque Applicatione.
XXXIX. Canones 2236-2240. De Pœnarum Remissione.
XL. Canones 2306-2313. De Remediis Pœnalibus et Pœnitentiis.

De Iure Romano

XLI. The Periods of Roman Law.
XLII. The *Corpus Iuris Civilis*—its Sources and Divisions.
XLIII. The Elements of Personality.
XLIV. The Manner of acquiring Roman Citizenship.
XLV. The Juridical Position of Women.
XLVI. The Roman Family.
XLVII. *Res Mancipi* and *Res nec Mancipi.*
XLVIII. Slavery.
XLIX. Manumission.
L. The Roman Conception of Marriage.
LI. *De Iure Postliminii.*
LII. *De Rerum Divisione et quomodo Res acquirantur.*

De Iure Internationali

LIII. Nature of International Law.
LIV. Sources of International Law.
LV. Conditions of State Existence.
LVI. Protectorates, Suzerainties, Mandates.
LVII. The Monroe Doctrine and American Policies.
XVIII. Jurisdiction of Rivers.
LIX. Diplomatic Agents.
LX. The Negotiation of Treaties.

* * * * * *

Vidit Facultas Iuris Canonici:

Philippus Bernardini, S.T.D., I.U.D., *Decanus.*
Ludovicus H. Motry, S.T.D., I.C.D., *a Secretis.*

Vidit Rector Universitatis:

✠ Thomas J. Shahan, S.T.D., I.U.L., LL.D.

VITA

Nicholas Martin Bliley was born in Richmond, Virginia, on December 6, 1893. He received his primary education in St. Ignatius School, a private Catholic school in Chesterfield County, Virginia, and his secondary education at Belmont Abbey College, Belmont, North Carolina. On June 24, 1911, he was invested with the habit of the Order of St. Benedict, and, after a year of probation, was admitted to simple perpetual profession on June 24, 1912. Three years later on July 11, 1915, he made his solemn profession as a monk of St. Benedict. His philosophical and theological studies were made in Belmont Abbey Seminary under the able direction of the late Bishop Haid, O. S. B., Vicar Apostolic of the vicariate of North Carolina and Abbot-Ordinary of Belmont Abbey.

He was ordained to the sacred priesthood by Bishop Haid, O. S. B., on June 3, 1917. For the next eight years he was engaged in teaching in the high school department of Belmont Abbey College. From January 1, 1923, to August 20, 1925, he was also the procurator of Belmont Abbey. In September, 1925, he matriculated at the Catholic University at Washington, and registered in the School of Canon Law. At the close of the academic year of 1925-1926, the degrees of Bachelor and Licentiate in Canon Law were conferred upon him. In partial fulfillment of the requirements for the degree of Doctor in Canon Law, he wrote and published this dissertation on Altars in accordance with the canonical and liturgical laws of the Church.

www.ingramcontent.com/pod-product-compliance
Lightning Source LLC
LaVergne TN
LVHW050212080826
844660LV00012B/400

9780813222271